Because of His Blood

by

Thelma Juanita Leftwich

DORRANCE PUBLISHING CO., INC.
PITTSBURGH, PENNSYLVANIA 15222

All Bible verses are taken from the King James Version.

ISBN # 0-8059-5006-0
Printed in the United States of America

First Printing

For information or to order additional books, please write:
Dorrance Publishing Co., Inc.
643 Smithfield Street
Pittsburgh, Pennsylvania 15222
U.S.A.
1-800-788-7654
Or visit our web site and on-line catalog at
www.dorrancepublishing.com.

To my husband, Otis, my John the Baptist, who told me:
"You must get this message on the Blood of Jesus into book form."

Contents

Preface

Over a decade has passed since the Lord assigned me to travel throughout the Body of Christ and teach on the Blood of Jesus. I formerly felt I needed a new message because I assumed people had already heard the teaching on the Precious Blood of Christ, but the Spirit of God would not release me and constantly affirmed that God wants His people to know what the Blood is all about. Jesus is coming for a perfect church; what is referred to as "His bride without spot, wrinkle, or blemish." But first much preparatory work must be done.

For many years the church has been dormant and unaware of the power at her disposal. I liken the church to a sleeping giant that has allowed the enemy to run over and deceive her. Many Christians have entered into God's salvation plan and never pushed any deeper into the provisions of God. It is time to rise up and defy the enemy through the Blood of Jesus.

God did not save us just to live a passive life and then take us into heaven when we die. He left us in this world because He has a job for each of us. We want to be doing the work of the Father with the power Jesus has given us. God does require us to "occupy" as we live here on this earth, so let us change our talk of just "making it in" through heaven's gate and work toward accomplishing things for God's kingdom on this earth.

Acknowledgments

To my son Devin Leftwich who proofread the manuscript.

To my son Brett Leftwich who typed the manuscript and showed me how to use the computer.

To my daughter Shawn Leftwich, who listened to my cries while waiting for publication.

To The Vessels of His Love Church family and all those who listened to me preach the Blood over and over again.

Chapter One

Why the Blood Was Given

After I first discovered the significance of the Blood of Christ in our Christian lives, I happened to watch a morning talk show that featured a former witch. As I heard her talk about the reality of Satan and demons in America today, I realized that people in the Third World countries are more educated on the reality of demonic activity than people in America. They understand that Satan is real and active on Earth today. She said everyone who joined Satan's ranks did so because they wanted power: They shed blood and offered sacrifices because they expected to receive power.

According to this former witch, witches would place assignments against people and especially enjoyed their assignments against Christians. They were amazed at how many church people did not know the power they had available to them. But more significant were her words about those who did understand the power of the Blood: "When we found a Christian who understood the power of the Blood in his heart and spoke the Blood of Jesus against us, we were literally paralyzed in our activities against him."

A. Why the Enemy Hides Truth

Satan wants power over our lives, but he cannot have it unless we give it to him. God has given us authority over Satan. The enemy cannot cross the Blood line that a knowledgeable Christian puts out there, and he puts that Blood line there by speaking "the Blood of Jesus." Speaking the Blood of Jesus over your life, your home, your family, and your possessions is not just a religious term. I believe, according to the Bible, you can speak interference and obstruction to the enemy's plan and keep him at bay in your life. God made His plan for victory simple through the means of a Blood covenant with Him. We do not have to go through fancy rituals or animal sacrifices practiced by many cultures in order to appease our God.

Spiritual warfare erupts because Satan wants your body. God is a Spirit and can only carry out His work on earth through willing bodies. That is why Romans 12:1 says to make your body a living sacrifice so God can manifest Himself through you. "I beseech you therefore, brethren, by the mercies of God, that ye present your bodies a living sacrifice, holy, acceptable unto God, which is your reasonable service." In the same way, Satan as a spiritual being has no power on the earth unless he can use a body. This reality is revealed in the Bible story of the man with the legion of demons. The devils pleaded with Jesus to give them another body when He cast them out:

> And when he was come to the other side into the country of the Gergesenes, there met him two possessed with devils, coming out of the tombs, exceeding fierce, so that no man might pass by that way. And behold, they cried out, saying, What have we to do with thee, Jesus, thou Son of God? Art thou come hither to torment us before the time? And there was a good way off from them an herd of many swine feeding. So the devils besought him, saying, "If thou cast us out, suffer us to go away into the herd of swine." And He said unto them, Go. And when they were come out, they went into the herd of swine: and, behold, the whole herd of swine ran violently down a steep place into the sea, and perished in the waters." (Matthew 8:28-32)

Satan understands many aspects of the Word of God that we too need to understand. If we take the authority that God gives us, we could stand up against the enemy. Do you know you have an enemy that brings obstacles against you in order to steal the Word sown in your heart? Just as in biblical times, Satan is still after the Word of God who is Jesus Christ. He wants as many people as he can get to go to hell with him when his time is up on this earth. If you don't cling to the Word of God and His principles and allow the Spirit of God to minister life to you, the enemy will trap you. There is no sidestepping eternal principles. If a person accepts Jesus, his future home will be heaven. If a person refuses Jesus Christ, his eternal home is hell.

B. End Time Weaponry

In the end times, we need the weapons that can counter what the enemy is doing. Satan does not have authentic power. He uses power gained through trickery. He uses the power invested in us as we allow him. He wants to keep us from realizing the power given in the Great Commission:

> And Jesus came and spake unto them, saying, All power is given unto me in heaven and in earth. Go ye therefore, and teach all nations, baptizing them in the Name of the Father and of the Son, and of the Holy Ghost: Teaching them to observe all things whatsoever I have commanded you: and, lo, I am with you always, even unto the end of the world. Amen. (Matthew 28:18-20)

With the power He invested in you, Jesus wants you to go into the world and do the works that He did. Satan knows he does not have any authority except when Christians allow him to use what belongs to them because they did not use their power. That is why we have to stand up and use what God's Word has given us. That is why God gives us the weapon of the Blood of Jesus.

C. Satan's Deceptions

Satan has deceived the church because he does not want the Body of Christ to know the power available to them. He has tried several diversions. He wants Christians to operate under the idea that the Heavenly Father puts harmful things on His people. He comes in disguise and attributes things such as sickness and suffering to the Heavenly Father. He hides the truth of John 10:10: "The thief cometh not but for to steal, and to kill, and to destroy: I am come that they might have life, and that they might have it more abundantly."

If you fail to identify the enemy, you will not fight; you will take everything that comes your way and think God is subjecting you to difficult situations. The church has been like a sleeping giant which does not understand the true nature and character of God. Although there are many gods in this world, there is only one true and living God. There is joy and power in serving Him. He took the same power that raised Jesus from the dead and placed it within us, yet we do not act as if we have power.

In order to usher in the final revival in the end times, we have an assignment to finish. We have to understand what God has given us. We are sitting on spiritual dynamite. The power in the Blood of Jesus is like an end time nuclear warhead and will usher in a revival. I believe true revival can only be marked by a knowledge of the power in the Blood of Jesus.

Another tactic of the enemy is to bring in counterfeit truth. I had a friend who used to work in a bank and was taught how to identify counterfeit money. The bank did not bring in counterfeit money to train employees how to identify it, the employees carefully studied real money so they could recognize a counterfeit bill when they saw it. In the same way, you need to read the Bible for yourself so you cannot be fooled by counterfeit information. If you know the Word of God, you will know how to expose the counterfeit immediately.

D. Critical Times

You are in a critical time of history and Satan as a roaring lion seeks whom he can destroy. He is a deceitful liar and will deceive even the elect. Many churchgoing people who are not deeply rooted in the Bible are being sucked in by false doctrine. One pastor asked his congregation how many people loved the Lord and also embraced the New Age theory. Half the congregation raised their hands. The New Age movement which has found its way into government, schools, politics, and religion has a stronghold. Why? Because people eloquent with words say things that sound like the Bible.

If Satan is going to deceive you, he is smart enough not to say something exactly opposite of God's truth. He will use something that sounds like the Bible. Many cults talk about Jesus as a philosopher, a lover of mankind, and a good man, but they will not say Jesus is the Son of God. The question to distinguish between truth and error is, "What do you do with Jesus?" Do you believe that He is God? There is only one way to God and that is through Jesus. "I am the door: by me if any man enter in, he shall be saved, and shall go in and out, and find pasture." (John 10:9) Jesus also said: "I am the way, the truth and the life; no man cometh unto the Father, but by me." (John 14:6)

One popular talk show featured a teacher who wrote a book about love and how to be a vessel of love. She talked about how God is in us which in turn makes us a god. She sounded impressive but did not identify Jesus Christ as the cornerstone of her teaching. I know many preachers who sound spiritual by talking about good living and being good to your neighbor, yet they never build the foundation that says, "Jesus Christ is the Son of God who came in the flesh and shed His Blood to redeem us. He is the second of the three persons of the Godhead." The enemy is deceiving and lying to the Body of Christ by taking everything holy and making a mockery of it. Satan is a real spirit being on this earth and deceives people by making them think he does not exist. If a thief comes into your home and steals all your possessions, it would be wonderful for the thief if you said, "There isn't any thief. I don't believe in thieves." That is what the enemy is doing to the church, coming right in before our eyes and robbing, killing, and destroying, while we stand by saying, "There isn't a devil. It must be God doing these bad things to me."

Once you start attending to God's Word and hiding it in you heart, the enemy will try to hinder you. For this reason you need to learn your authority and pray against the hindering forces and spirits and come into what God has promised you. When you go after the Word, lift up the Blood of Jesus on your banner. Isaiah 54:17 will prove true in your life:

> No weapon that is formed against thee shall prosper; and every tongue that shall rise against thee in judgment thou shalt condemn. This is the heritage of the servants of the Lord, and their righteousness is of me, saith the Lord.

The scripture says there may be weapons against you, but they will not prosper. Know who your enemy is and who is the giver of every good gift. The devil does not care if you go to church and sit on a pew as long as you do not understand the weapons in your arsenal. Go and pick up the nuclear bomb of the Blood of Jesus by gaining an understanding of what the Blood does for you. Make it a part of your life and begin to act on the understanding you have sown in your heart.

E. Gaining Understanding

For many years as a Christian, I did not understand what the Blood was about until I studied God's Word for myself. A person can be deceived unless they personally know God's Word. One person told me, "You better carry your Bible around and wear it like you wear shoes. It is a necessary part of your dress." In this day and time, you will be deceived unless you know what the Spirit of God is saying to the Body of Christ. You have to read your Bible and gather in an assembly with other Christians. The Spirit of God moves though His Word and Spirit and these two will always agree.

Just as God told Israel that He wanted to bring them into the land of milk and honey so all nations would know He chose them, God today wants to bring out His children and give them good and perfect gifts. He wants to be a God of provision today. His requirement is that we do not have any gods before Him. We cannot be like the children of Israel who witnessed miracles and crossed the Red Sea with promises of "Yes, Lord, whatever You want from us." How soon they forgot God and His goodness! They willfully chose not to remember Him as they began to seek other gods.

God sent Himself in the form of a man who died on the cross to redeem us and give us right standing with Him. He has, by his Blood, opened the way into His throne room so we can come boldly before Him and receive His mercy whenever we need it. It is His pleasure to give you abundant life. When you gain an understanding of what the Blood of Jesus has done and what it can do in your life, you will never be the same. It is an "alive" Blood that has not lost its power.

F. Life of the Flesh in the Blood

What makes the Blood of Jesus so important? A fundamental scripture is found in Leviticus 17:11. "For the life of the flesh is in the Blood: and I have given it to you upon the altar to make an atonement for your souls: for it is the Blood that maketh an atonement for the soul." Jesus has prepared the way for us to be holy by His Blood.

As a former high school science teacher, I was excited by the first truth found in this scripture. It reveals a number one fact—the life of the flesh is in the Blood. When I think about the blood and its importance in the human body, I know we would not be living if it was not for the blood. The blood is the transportation system that carries everything the body requires since the organs in the body do not move around in the body.

As important as the blood is to the body it cannot sustain life without oxygen. Oxygen is more important than food or water. You breathe oxygen in through your nose and mouth into your lungs. It then passes into the blood which takes it around to all of the organs. This life sustaining element is flowing in the blood. You need a steady and constant supply of oxygen or else your cells will die. Brain cells that die cannot be replaced. When a heart stops beating, it is not because of the blood: a person dies because the oxygen cannot get around the body through the blood. Oxygen breathed into the system brings life in the blood.

The same law applies in the spiritual realm. When God, who is a Spirit, created man in His own image and likeness, He created man to be a spirit being. Genesis 2:7 says, "And the Lord God formed man of the dust of the ground, and breathed into his nostrils the breath of life; and man became a living soul." When God breathed into man, He gave him life unlike any other animal. All animals have biological life, but man was given more than just biological life. He was given what in the Greek is called "Zoe" life, which means the God-kind of life.

Adam entered into the spiritual realm at the point the life of God was placed within him. His biological life was not only oxygenated, but his spiritual life was animated with God's life. As God breathed life into Adam, that breath traveled into his spiritual blood system. Adam was given the same quality of life God had and was made to be like God. At this point, Adam lived in utopia in the Garden of Eden because He had God's life and blood. He was a replica of His Heavenly Father although he was given a body so he could relate to an earthly environment.

Whatever you put in the blood travels to all parts of the body. The blood is responsible for communicating to every cell in the body. Whatever you need to sustain life is in the blood. If you put anything harmful into the blood like drugs, it will go to all the cells of the body. That is why it is such a destructive trick of the enemy to bring drugs into our culture, and why John 10:10 says, "The thief cometh not, but for to steal, and to kill, and to destroy...."

The blood system that gives life also picks up the waste products spilled back into the blood when the cells have used food. This compares to our life in Jesus Christ. We are the Body of Christ, and Jesus, who is our Blood, allows every member or cell in the Body of Christ to be in constant communication with Him. He brings life to the Blood and cleanses us of all the waste products in our lives.

The three vessels in the body known as the arteries, veins, and capillaries can be compared to the spiritual church. Arteries that carry blood away from the heart are like the five-fold ministry which carries the life in God's Word to the Body of Christ. The veins that carry blood to the heart are the intercessors who carry the petitions of people back to the heart of the Heavenly Father. The capillaries that exchange materials in the blood are the net workers. These are the missionaries who go out where the work takes place and exchange the life of God for the people's sin, sickness, and sadness.

6

G. Cleansing Power of the Blood

The cleansing power of the blood is amazing. If you experiment with a tourniquet on your arm, you will notice extreme pain in your arm when you exercise it with the tourniquet tightened. This happens because the tourniquet stops circulation. Every time you work or expend energy, waste products and carbon dioxide are released. As soon as you loosen the tourniquet and let the blood flow, you cleanse the area of waste material.

Physiologists relate how blood cells enter into the two million coils in the kidneys and cleanse out the waste products back through the blood. Every single cell is dealt with in the many coils of the kidneys as one gallon of blood is pumped from the heart every second. This is just how the Blood of Jesus operates. There are waste products or rubbish in people's lives called sin. This sin will cause eternal death in a body if it is not cleansed by the Blood of Jesus. His Blood cleanses the body of sin. The Blood has to be flowing in people's lives in order to keep them cleansed.

H. Unity

God is very consistent. The laws He made in the physical realm also apply in the spiritual realm. The Lord designed the Body of Christ to work in the same manner as the physical body. It is important for Christians to learn to work together. If they are not functioning the way they should, they are living in a sick body. God used the example of a body so we could understand that just as bodily organs function together, different parts of the Body of Christ should function together. We need to work together so He can come for a perfect church.

Look at your body. The blood takes oxygen and food to all the cells and carries away carbon dioxide from the cells. No one organ or system works independently. The digestive system does not say, "I don't want your services, blood; I will deliver my own food." The digestive system has to give up its food to the circulatory system so the blood can carry it. All the organs and systems have to work together in order to make a well-functioning organism.

I. Immunity

The blood is so powerful that when disease enters in, the whole body is affected. If body cells begin fighting each other, then you will have a diseased condition. If the Body of Christ fights against one another and does not work cooperatively, they cannot be the perfect bride and perfect body that God intended. The circulatory system contains three types of blood cells: red blood cells which carry oxygen, white blood cells which are the army that stand up and fight off invaders that enter the body, and antibodies that cause a body to build up an immunity once it has been infected. The immune system is a built-in system whose purpose is to take care of the works of the enemy. The blood has enemies or viruses that try to affect the body, but the trillions of white blood cells produced in the bone marrow work to identify the enemy.

There are three kind of white blood cells. The one called the phagocyte is a cell-eater that eats up viruses that come into the body. The t-cell or helper cells are alerted of an invasion in the body by the phagocyte. Although the phagocyte is eating as many enemies as possible, there may be a time when it tells the t-cells to help. The t-cells then go to the spleen and lymph nodes and cause them to produce more white cells which are killer t-cells. If the virus has attacked a cell, the killer t-cell will pierce that cell and cause it to spill out the virus so that the virus cannot do deadly harm to that cell. This action stimulates cells called b-cells which begin chemical warfare. More antibodies are produced so that bad cells cannot get by them. They attach themselves to the cell invading the body and neutralize that cell in such a way that whenever another cell of that nature enters into the system, they are identified. The b-cells and t-cells float around the body for years standing guard against any cells that are similar to what they have defeated before. When another virus comes in, these cells say, "We have your number. You are not getting past the front line of our forces."

God designed a similar immunity system in the spiritual realm. When invaders enter your life, you tell them you have the Blood of Jesus and the "spiritual t-cells" will start working. The return attack of the enemy is identified. You can use God's word which says in Nahum 1:96, "Affliction shall not rise up the second time."

J. Importance of Blood Today

God loves His bride, which is the Body of Christ. You need to know God loves you and has His heart set upon you. Just as God wants to give you a revelation of the importance of His Blood, Satan wants to keep you blinded as to what you possess with the Blood. Understanding the Blood gives you everything you need to be victorious in this world.

When Jesus said, "It is finished" on the cross, He poured every provision you need into your life. It is when we do not appropriate the promises for ourselves that the devil has an advantage over us. We give him our authority when we do not use our authority against him. Satan looks to see if we are going to give him authority to do what he wants. If he sees you armed with the Word of God and the Blood, there is not a thing he can do against you. But if he can keep you defeated and weak, he will do it.

If you believe in your heart and confess with your mouth that you are protected by the Blood of Jesus, you will be. You have that right because Jesus took His Blood and sprinkled it over the heavenly tabernacle. According to Hebrews 4:16, "Let us therefore come boldly unto the throne of grace that we may obtain mercy, and find grace to help in time of need," and Hebrews 12:24, "…and to the blood of sprinkling, that speaketh better things than that of Abel," the Blood of Jesus still speaks today and when God the Father looks at the Blood, He knows we are forgiven through the sacrifice of Jesus. The enemy looks at the Blood and knows it puts him to public shame.

You have to believe the Blood has power. Satan should not be having a harvest in our homes because we have not taken authority. If we will stand up individually and united as the Body of Christ, we will regain power. In past years, the church has allowed its position in the world to decrease in power. Secular society should be looking to the church to see what they should do, but instead the church has backed off. The church has started conforming to the world and allowed the world to show us what to do. I believe the Spirit of God is saying "enough is enough."

If we don't take the Word in its fullness and understand the completed work Jesus did on the cross, it is like slapping Jesus in the face and saying, "Everything you have done means nothing." If Jesus came to earth to shed His Blood and we do not take advantage of this fact, it is our fault. He gave His Blood for life, for cleansing, for protection, and for healing.

If you are in the family of God and have entered into the kingdom through accepting the Blood of Jesus Christ, then God is your Father; He is not just "the man upstairs," but He is your Heavenly Father. He is a God of love and all that He does comes out of love. Love is the nature and character of our Father. As you grow in a revelation of this love, then the world will know what He means to you. They will see the reality on your face and in your life.

God wants to establish you in love and power because He is looking for powerhouses to represent Him. I believe we are coming into the day and season when the focus will not be on the big name preachers and teachers, it will be on the ordinary people around us. God is willing to use whoever is willing to do what He says.

Sometimes we look at our own personal flaws and shortcomings and forget that God looks right past the faults and looks into our hearts. He hears the cries for mercy and the cries to be a vessel used by Him. I was inspired by a teaching by Myles Monroe, a pastor/teacher from the Bahamas, who exclaimed how he did not want anything that is important to the kingdom of God to go with him when he went to the grave; he wanted everything God had implanted in him to be spilled out in this life. What an important revelation. We must fulfill what God has given us to do on this earth and see that God is not yet finished with us.

Chapter Two

The Journey of the Blood

In the beginning God created the heavens and the earth. And the earth was without form and void; and darkness was upon the face of the deep. And the Spirit of God moved upon the face of the waters." (Genesis 1:1-2) Even though God has no beginning and no ending, the beginning refers to what we can measure as time. God is timeless but gives time to us so we have something to which we can relate.

As we travel back to the beginning of time, we see God creating the heavens and earth. When something is created, it is taken from nothing in order to get something. When God created the world, the earth was void; He created by starting with nothing. God is the only One able to create. We can never create anything new. Man can only make or discover something from what already exists.

Every father wants a child of whom he can be proud so he can say, "That child is just like me." God had the same desire when He created us in His image and likeness. He wanted our fellowship. That is why it is important to understand how much you mean to God. Your preciousness in His sight is clearly reflected in the story of creation.

It was on the sixth day that God created Adam. He wanted to create a man after His image and likeness. In order to have man like Him, He had to create man as a spiritual being. So He created the spirit of man by speaking out of Himself. When God speaks, things happen. He now had a beautiful world and the spirit of man but needed someone to take care of the earth. This new creation of man had to be especially equipped with an earth suit in order to live in the world. Notice in Genesis 2:7 how God reached down into the dust of the earth which is something that already existed, and formed man. "And the Lord God formed man of the dust of the ground, and breathed into his nostrils the breath of life; and man became a living soul."

The whole creation was made for man in order to be pleasing to him. God did creation in a beautiful way because man was the only one to be in charge of the earth. He wanted earth to be like heaven which is reflected in the Lord's Prayer; "Thy kingdom come. Thy will be done in earth, as it is in heaven." (Matthew 6:10) God had established heaven and wanted to make a home for man that would duplicate His home. He was a good God making good things.

Adam was different from any other creature. God first formed Adam which gave him the biological life common to the other animals. But He gave more than physical life to Adam. No other animal on earth was given the breath of life that man was given. "And the Lord God formed man of the dust of the ground, and breathed into his nostrils the breath of life; and man became a living soul." (Genesis 2:7) God breathed into him His own nature which caused man to become a living soul. Man now had the same life in his blood as God. Adam also was different from other animals because he could choose whom to serve and obey.

Adam was also given dominion. According to Genesis 1:28, man's dominion was total. And God blessed them, and God said unto them, "Be fruitful and multiply, and replenish the earth, and subdue it: and have dominion over the fish of the sea, and over the fowl of the air, and over every living thing that moveth upon the earth." Once God speaks something, He does not go back on His word. He cannot take back the dominion He has given man. God even brought the animals to Adam so he could name them. I often imagine a dialogue which would capture the conversation between God and Adam.

"Look, Adam, I created the sky, moon and stars. What do you think?" God said.

"They are good," replied Adam.

"Look at my vegetation and my animals," God said.

"They are good, too. But, Lord, I noticed one thing that is not good. Every male has a female. You created me in your image and I do not have a counterpart nor do you," questioned Adam.

"It is not good for man to dwell alone, Adam. I knew you would understand the need for a counterpart. Now I want to show you a principle that will endure from this time on."

God wanted to teach Adam the principle found in John 12:24. "Verily, verily, I say unto you, except a corn of wheat fall into the ground and die, it abideth alone; but if it die, it bringeth forth much fruit." As a type of Jesus, Adam had to lay down his life in order to receive life in the form of Eve. In the same way Jesus laid down His life to receive us. God's principles in the spiritual realm parallel principles in the natural realm. In vegetative life, seeds must fall to the ground and die to bring forth new life. In the same way, He wanted Adam to be like a corn of wheat that goes into a deathlike state to bring forth fruit.

I imagine God then explained to Adam, "You have to agree to be that corn of wheat and go into a deathlike state to bring fruit, Adam; I cannot create anymore because creation is over and My Word said I cannot create anything new. I said I will no longer do any work because I have ceased from my labor. But as you go into a deathlike state, I will bring forth the second life which will complete you."

Just as we learned that the life of the flesh is in the blood in Leviticus 17:11, we now learn that the life of a plant is in its seed. From the plant to the animal world, there has to be a seed in order to be fruitful and multiply.

A. Creation of Eve

God then caused Adam to sleep. "And the Lord God caused a deep sleep to fall upon Adam, and he slept: and he took one of his ribs, and closed up the flesh instead thereof. And the rib, which the Lord God had taken from man, made he a woman, and brought her unto the man." (Genesis 2:21-22).

When God reached into Adam, a seed was already planted. God already had what He needed to bring forth and build upon. Eve was not a new creation. She was already in Adam. God only had to reach inside and bring the seed forth in order to form Eve. God reached into Adam, built on the seed and created for him the beautiful creature called woman. The Bible says He molded, fashioned, and delicately formed the woman. He didn't just throw a hunk of dirt together!

Adam was well pleased with Eve because he had his counterpart. Adam and Eve were now complete and one in the garden. When God told them to keep the garden, the word "keep" can be defined in several ways. It was to be kept looking good and safe. But why couldn't the garden take care of itself? Obviously God had not taken darkness out of the world and man had to guard against that darkness. I believe this darkness represented the kingdom of Satan. I do not know if God explained to Adam that he had an enemy, a spirit being who needed a body to live on earth.

Genesis 1:2 reminds us, "And the earth was without form and void; and darkness was upon the face of the deep. And the Spirit of God moved upon the face of the waters." Darkness has nothing to do with God because He is the light of men. Darkness is the opposite of light. Heaven is described as a place with neither darkness nor shadows. We see in Genesis 1:5 that light and darkness were divided. "And God called the light Day, and the darkness he called Night. And the evening and the morning were the first day."

B. Fall of Adam and Eve

God warned Adam not to eat from the tree of the knowledge of good and evil or else he and his mate would die. God is not a controller; He will not make man do anything. Man could either allow God to be the light and life in his body or allow the enemy to be what filled his life. When Eve was deceived by the darkness that came in the shape of a serpent, they failed the test God gave them.

But why did Satan need a body in which to manifest himself? One of the rules of earth is that no creature can live on the earth without a body. Spirit beings need a body. Satan still needs a body even today. He needs a legal residence on earth to move in the way he wants. Judas, the disciple who betrayed Jesus, did not do anything until the devil entered into him. That is why we have spiritual warfare today: a. God needs a body to manifest Himself in the earth and Satan needs one as well. b. Satan had a legal right on earth once he had a body in the form of a serpent. c. There is a war going on for the human body. d. The question is: Who gets the body?

The moment Adam and Eve ate the fruit of the forbidden tree, they became one with that darkness. God would not step in at this point and stop Eve from eating the fruit because He gave authority to man. Adam was the only one who could have stopped her, and he did not. As a result, they disconnected their power plug into the spirit realm. Adam put out his light and severed himself from God. Let us go back and see how this can happen.

C. Circulating Death

The only way you can cause something to circulate through the body is to put it into the blood system so it spreads to all the body. Just as oxygen enters the blood and gives life to all parts of the body, when God breathed life into Adam, He placed life in his blood system. God told Adam as long as he obeyed God, he would have life. It was his choice. If Adam did not obey, death was promised to him. When sin entered into their bodies, death began to take place. As long as God's life was in his body, Adam was living a God-kind of life. But when death came, it spread throughout his system and Adam began to die.

Even today we can see this system of death working in our bodies. By coming into the world, we are destined to die a physical death. Cells begin to die—some replenish themselves and some do not. Adam began to die because of the pollution in his blood. Since Adam was the first man, and we all descended from Adam, we have received his polluted blood. We come into this life with sin in our blood.

Adam and Eve were made without sin and had the opportunity to go through eternity sinless, but through their choice, Adam and Eve were no longer one with God and could not stand in His presence. They became aware of that fact and tried to cover themselves with leaves. They recognized their nakedness and sinfulness. According to Hebrews 9:22, blood has to be shed to remit sins. "And almost all things are by the law purged with blood; and without shedding of blood is no remission." Not even leaves could cover their sin and nakedness as God begins to reveal His plan about the importance of shedding blood. He laid the foundation for teaching the importance of the blood by killing an animal and shedding its blood for the animal skins that temporarily covered Adam and Eve in their sinful nakedness.

Adam allowed darkness to come in. When he ate that fruit, it became a part of him because he ate from the kingdom of darkness. Instead of the life of God controlling his system, darkness, which is light absent, controlled him. Darkness and light cannot occupy the same area. Because Adam disconnected himself from God who was the power source, the Old Testament people had to wait for reconnection to God. This could only happen when Jesus would come. Man had a debt he could not pay; Jesus paid the bill and had man's lights turned back on.

13

Everything in the Old Testament is a type and similitude of what is in the New Testament. Old Testament people walked in darkness because the Spirit could not communicate with them due to their polluted blood. God would talk to men through priests, kings or prophets, but until Jesus came they could not know God. They only feared him as Someone awesome who would consume them.

All of the Old Testament blood sacrifices related the importance of blood for the remission of sins. Blood is even more important than the heart that pumps it. If there is no blood, there is no life. An unfertilized egg has no life in it until the blood begins to form, which happens upon fertilization. Eggs have not blood without fertilization. If there is blood, there is life. We have no spiritual life until His life is in our blood system.

Even though it seemed like Satan had the advantage after deceiving Adam and Eve, God made a promise when he cursed the serpent Satan had inhabited. Genesis 3:14-15 promises,

> And the Lord God said unto the serpent, Because thou hast done this, thou are cursed above all cattle, and above every beast of the field; upon thy belly shalt thou go, and dust shalt thou eat all the days of thy life: And I will put enmity between thee and the woman, and between thy seed and her seed; it shall bruise thy head, and thou shalt bruise his heel.

Did you wonder why God cursed the serpent? God was essentially saying in Genesis 3:14-15, "Satan, you think you have Me now, but I am cursing the body that gave you legal right on earth. I promise you, Satan, I will establish a Seed on earth through a woman. You will bruise the heel of this Seed but this Seed will crush your head." God was not dumbfounded by what occurred in the Garden because He still had a plan. That Seed of the woman was Jesus. Just as Satan legally operated through the body of a serpent, God was going to legally bring into the world His Son through a woman's body. And God was saying, "You may bruise the heel of Jesus Christ but He will crush your head."

We will discover the importance of God's timing. He does not do something just because of an immediate need. Even though man needed a blood transfusion after Adam and Eve's sin, God needed a time of preparation. If He rescued man immediately, man would have done the same thing again. It took 4,000 years for God to bring His plan to fruition. All through that time He had to find the people who would trust Him and stand up for Him. When the stage was set, everything in place, then, "When the fullness of time had come, God sent forth His Son, born of a woman, born under the law." (Galatians 4:4)

Chapter Three

Pure Blood Stolen

When something is polluted, that object is made unclean, impure, or defiled; it is actually contaminated. God never desired for Adam and Eve to sin and fall out of His presence, but once they did, He had no choice but to exile them.

We see how Adam, who had a perfect system with God's pure blood flowing in his veins, permitted pollution to enter his system through disobedience. Because life is in the blood, his Godlike blood became polluted when he sinned. Death came upon him and took the place of life. His death was not instantaneous, but gradual. Spiritual death was taking place over a process of time with physical death as the result. When death completed its course, Adam died.

Just as we pass our blood line down to our children when we reproduce, Adam passed his polluted blood to his offspring. That is why every person born of Adam has polluted blood. Sin is in our nature. We are born into the world of sin not because of direct actions on our part, but because we have received our blood from Adam.

God realized He had to change corruptible blood into incorruptible blood. How was He going to do that and still be fair? A man had introduced sin and death into the world, so only a man could redeem the world from it. But where in God's creation could God find a man with pure blood? Everybody else who came after Adam had Adam's polluted blood.

What was needed to get man free and give life again? The answer is a blood transfusion. God was aware of that need and addressed His desire for life in Ezekiel 16:6: "And when I passed by thee, and saw thee polluted in thine own blood, I said unto thee when thou was in thy blood, Live; yea, I said unto thee when thou was in thy blood, Live." This verse did not just refer to Israel but refers to us today. God saw us in our own polluted blood and had a plan to bring His life back into our blood. God's earnest desire is for us to live. Even at this point in history, the heart of the Father was crying out, "I do not want you to die, I want you to live. I have the perfect plan to bring you life, otherwise you will never have eternal life in your polluted state." From this point on it was God's sole intent and purpose to institute or put into motion a way for us to live again in the God-kind of life.

A. Corruptible Blood

What is the significance of Adam's blood being corruptible or contaminated? In Jewish communities, it was unlawful to eat meat with blood for two reasons: (1) the life of the flesh was in the blood, and (2) blood is corruptible. Blood has a characteristic of quick decomposition. In a short period of time, meat with blood would begin to become putrid.

In John chapter 11, when Lazarus was dead and his sister warned Jesus not to roll back the stone in front of the tomb, Jesus said, "Take ye away the stone." Martha, the sister of him that was dead, saith unto him, "Lord, by this time he stinketh: for he hath been dead four days." (John 11:39.) Since embalming was not practiced in that day, dead bodies with their corruptible blood would be overwhelmingly foul to be around. For this reason, our culture takes out the blood and puts a chemical in the blood vessels so the body will not decay so quickly. This is called embalming.

Understanding the corruptible nature of the blood makes the future incorruptible blood of Jesus quite significant. From the time Adam and Eve sinned in the Garden and God made garments from animal skins, blood had to be constantly shed to cover sin. Until the time of Jesus, animal blood was only a covering for sin and could never take sin away; it was just a temporary atonement so people could come into the presence of God.

B. The Role of the High Priest

Throughout the Old Testament the children of Israel knew not to eat blood because life was contained in the blood. When God ordained the tabernacle in the wilderness sacrifices were the only way the sins of the children of Israel could be covered. Blood sacrifices gave release from sin. We see the tabernacle as a symbol or shadow of what was in heaven. The tabernacle built in Moses's time was a place where the corruptible blood of animals ran over the altar. The stench must have been tremendous because of how quickly blood decomposes. Although many people think of the tabernacle as a beautiful place, it must have been like a slaughterhouse.

The tabernacle was divided into three sections—outer court, holy place, and holy of holies. Only the priest could enter the holy of holies after a ritual of cleansing and purification. This purification was necessary because that was where the presence of the Lord dwelled. God made it known what was required and that only blood could make atonement for sin.

The priest brought animal blood, but it was not yet the perfect sacrifice. Every year the high priest went into the holy of holies and sprinkled the mercy seat. All he could do was cover the children of Israel and himself for twelve months. He would present the blood and hold off the wrath of God for another year. Hebrews 9:7-12 explains this ritual:

16

> But into the second went the high priest alone once every year, not without blood, which he offered for himself, and for the errors of the people: The Holy Ghost this signifying, that the way into the holiest of all was not yet made manifest, while as the first tabernacle was yet standing: The Holy Ghost this signifying, that the way into the holiest of all was not yet made manifest, while as the first tabernacle was yet standing: Which was a figure for the time then present, in which were offered both gifts and sacrifices, that could not make him that did the service perfect, as pertaining to the conscience; Which stood only in meats and drinks, and divers washings, and carnal ordinances imposed on them until the time of reformation. But Christ being come an high priest of good things to come, by a greater and more perfect tabernacle, not made with hands, that is to say, not of this building; neither by the blood of goats and calves, but by his own Blood he entered in once into the holy place, having obtained eternal redemption for us.

Just as God requires of us today, the high priest had to be holy in that time. The priest wore a robe with bells that would tinkle as he moved around in the holy of holies. A rope was attached to his waist and extended out to the people. If the priest was not holy before the Lord, he would fall dead when he went in to offer sacrifices. The people knew if the bells stopped tinkling the priest was dead and needed to be pulled out with the rope.

Did God want to kill this high priest? No, but it grieved His heart for sin to come into His presence. Sin cannot stand in the presence of His holiness. The priest could not bring blood for sacrifice without purifying himself. The Old Testament sacrifices that involved corruptible blood showed the people what was necessary to deal with sin, but Old Testament people could not receive Him because they still had the blood of their father Adam. They could not receive God's love so God had to institute laws to be a "schoolteacher" to keep man in line until Jesus their Redeemer or Messiah could come and save them from the law's curse. Four hundred years passed between the time the Old Testament closed and the New Testament opened. During this time, God was teaching people that sins had to be covered by blood. God could not work in a polluted situation and blood was what covered sin.

A covering would have to be sufficient until Galatians 4:4-5 occurred: "But when the fullness of the time was come, God sent forth his Son, made of a woman, made under the law, to redeem them that were under the law, that we might receive the adoption of sons." The prophets prophesied about the Holy One of Israel, the perfect Lamb who would restore. All Israelites knew about Him. God was setting the stage so when Jesus came they would realize the fulfillment about which these prophets spoke. The lamb in the Old Testament pointed to Jesus.

C. Cain and Abel

Cain and Abel, the sons of Adam, came to the Lord to give sacrifices. Cain gave vegetables from his garden and Abel brought a lamb without spot and blemish. How did they know the importance of a sacrifice? I believe their father Adam taught them because he learned that lesson from the time the first animal sacrifice was made and he was covered with the skin of an animal. Only blood could give remission of sins. God received Abel's offering, but did not receive Cain's offering.

I used to think God wasn't fair by rejecting Cain's offering until I realized without the shedding of blood there was no remission of sins. Cain and Abel knew this because their father had taught them how to cover sin. Cain was like many of us. Even though God requires certain things of us, we decide to serve Him in our own religious way. Cain cold not make up his own program to serve the Lord, but only serve Him by the rules of the blood.

When God saw the vegetables, He essentially said, "This will not work. You are not bringing blood." Cain was enraged in his heart and said, "Why are you accepting Abel's sacrifice and not mine?" He became so angry over his rejected gift that he murdered his own brother. Genesis 4:9-10 reads, "And the Lord said unto Cain, Where is Abel thy brother? And he said, I know not: am I my brother's keeper?" And he said, "What hast thou done? The voice of thy brother's blood crieth unto me from the ground."

Abel's blood was alive and speaking, demanding vengeance on his murderer. His life was prematurely taken away and he wanted revenge. In the book of Revelation, we see the same situation where saints in heaven cry before the throne. "And they cried with a loud voice, saying, How long, O Lord, holy and true, dost thou not judge and avenge our blood on them that dwell on the earth? (Revelation 6:10). Although Abel's blood speaks, Hebrews 12:24 indicates the Blood of Jesus points to something even better. "And to Jesus the mediator of the new covenant, and to the Blood of sprinkling, that speaketh better things than that of Abel."

Abel's blood was crying out for revenge, but God is saying a better way has come. When Jesus sprinkled His Blood, it now cries out for God's mercy on the people. The Blood of Jesus is incorruptible Blood not polluted by the sin of Adam. His Blood did not putrefy at death, but ever lives in the throne room of heaven so God's people can have entrance into the presence of God. The ever-living Blood always says, "You are forgiven because I have mercy on you."

This Blood does more than cover sin; it removes sin. It cleanses. Filthy garments washed with red Blood will turn white when God washes away sin under the New Testament covenant.

D. Abraham and Isaac

God was pleased with Abraham because he believed God. When God told Abraham to come and give up his only son that he loved, Abraham was willing to sacrifice Isaac. But why would it say his "only" son when he had a son named Ishmael? Ishmael was the son of works—the product of what he and Sarah concocted to try to bring about God's promise of a child in their lives. Sarah told Abraham to have relations with the handmaiden Hagar because Sarah thought she was too old to bear a child. The result of that plan was Ishmael, who was a source of harassment from that time forward. Sarah even came to complain to Abraham about the problems Ishmael and Hagar were causing in the home. She was right in a spiritual context to see that things could not work out through Ishmael because God wanted to work through the son of promise.

Ishmael was Abraham's son, not Sarah's son. In a sense, God required him to sacrifice his natural son. We often must give up natural things before God can deal with us according to His spiritual promises. Ishmael was a product of their own works, a result of man's work. God loved Ishmael and still loved Abraham and Sarah even though they took things into their own hands, but God had a divine order and a son of promise He wanted to bring about. Having separated Ishmael and Hagar from Abraham's presence, God could refer to Isaac as an only son of Abraham.

God operates differently than we do. People will often disagree when you do what God says. You cannot always please men or explain to them about God's way in your life. Obedience is the most important thing once you know God has spoken. So when God finally manifested Isaac, Abraham was ready to sacrifice the only son of promise. He had already sacrificed natural things and was ready to sacrifice spiritual things. Some of us are never able to see what God has for us until we give up our natural securities and arrangements.

In obedience to God, Abraham rose early in the morning without hesitation. He did not try to wait on God to see if He would change His mind. He did what God said and never once uttered a negative word about this test he was about to go through. He gathered his servants, his son, and a bundle of wood to use in burning the sacrifice. Abraham was resting in the fact that God had a covenant with Him. God would not break the covenant because He is faithful.

When Abraham and Isaac came to Mount Moriah, Isaac innocently asked, "Father, where is the lamb for sacrifice?" Abraham said, "God will provide Himself a lamb for a burnt offering." Even if the knife lifted over his son killed Isaac, Abraham knew God would perform a miracle because of His promises. He did not look at the circumstances and knew that everything would turn out right in the end. God was not—and still is not—a covenant-breaking God.

As the knife was about to plunge, God said, "Stop." Abraham believed and obeyed God through his willingness to sacrifice his only spiritual son. This spiritual sacrifice was pleasing to God and the sacrifice God really wanted.

God had now in Abraham a man of faith; a man with whom He could establish a blood covenant; a man through whom He could, under the law, establish a blood line through which He could bring forth the Redeemer. Through Abraham's blood line, God would bring forth His only Son.

Chapter Four

God's Restoration

God knew He needed a man with "God's life" in him in order to complete His plan of redemption. He needed someone to replace Adam, but had to do it in a legal way because He is a just God. He had to bring a man to redeem what the original man had lost. He had begun this plan before the foundation of the earth.

A. God Prepares a Body

God began to work out His plan through a young girl named Mary, who was probably around fourteen years old at the time. In Biblical time, it was common for girls to marry young. Mary was engaged to be married to Joseph when the angel Gabriel came to Mary and spoke:

> And the angel came in unto her, and said, "Hail, thou that art highly favored, the Lord is with thee: blessed art thou among women." And when she saw him, she was troubled at his saying, and cast in her mind what manner of salutation this should be. And the angel said unto her, "Fear not, Mary; for thou hast found favor with God. And, behold, thou shalt conceive in thy womb, and bring forth a son, and shalt call His name Jesus." (Luke 1:28-31).

The Lord was requiring the same thing of Mary as He required of Adam in the Garden of Eden and what He was going to require of Jesus on the cross. He was asking her to lay down her life to fulfill the purposes of God. Her natural response was, "How can this come about without relations with a man?"

Perhaps God's thoughts were, *We do not want a man to have anything to do with this plan because we do not want polluted blood.* Even though she did not understand the full extent of the plan, her submissive response was: "Be it unto me according to your Word." She was saying that she was available to lay down her life. She was available and obedient and did not consider the ridicule or reproach that would come on her as people suspected she had committed fornication.

At that moment, I believe God breathed life into Mary's womb just as He breathed the breath of life into Adam. He was providing a man who could provide a blood transfusion because of the divinity within him. He needed a God-man. The entire Trinity came into focus at this conception. The Holy Spirit who does the work, overshadowed Mary's womb causing conception to take place and producing a child from the Blood of the Father—all man and all God—Jesus the Christ whose spirit had always existed, but now had an earthly body provided for Him.

We have to understand the process of human birth to realize the beauty of God's plan. Just as a chicken egg has no life unless a rooster fertilizes the egg, the egg of a woman has no life in it without fertilization by sperm. The sperm providing the beginning of blood in the egg means fertilization has occurred and life is present. The life of the flesh is in the blood. If there is no blood, there is no life. If you look into a microscope, an egg just fertilized would show little blood vessels being formed. Any egg with blood is a fertilized egg. Fertilization causes the blood to begin to flow.

Mary had an egg of human origin, but fertilization came by the Spirit of God, giving that egg divine Blood. When the Father by the Holy Spirit overshadowed the virgin Mary, the life of Jesus was put into her womb. The Old Testament prophesied that a body would be prepared for Jesus the man, so we can now realize how Jesus could be born as the Son of God and still inherit the characteristics needed to be called the Son of man.

Jesus was the Son of God by the Blood of the Father and the Son of man by the egg within Mary's body. It was totally necessary for Jesus to be born of a virgin. No human male was involved in the conception. Therefore, incorruptible blood was flowing in the veins of Jesus. At this point God is beginning to reveal what it means to give us a blood transfusion with the Blood that has eternal life in it. Zoe life, or "the God-kind of life," was about to enter the earth again.

God needed Mary's reproductive system, but He could not use her blood because she descended from Adam. He could not use man's blood because it was polluted. But would not Jesus be polluted by Mary's blood? No, it is a medical fact that blood from the fetus never crosses the placenta nor does the blood found in the embryo come from the woman's blood. A process of diffusion occurs through the placental wall, but never the passage of blood. Mary's blood never touched the blood of Jesus. There was a separating wall because of the structure of the placenta. Jesus was not polluted by Mary's human blood; neither was Mary made into a deity because of Jesus' Blood. That is why it is important we only esteem Mary as an obedient servant of God and not as one to worship. There are only three Persons in the Godhead, and Mary is not one of them.

It is also crucial that we never undermine the importance of the virgin birth. The only way a blood transfusion could be given to mankind to get us back into right standing with God was through the virgin birth. Jesus

22

Christ is true God and true man, and His birth brought a new line of Blood into the earth to redeem mankind from a sinful state.

B. Sinless Walk on Earth

We do not have much of an account of the life of Jesus apart from His birth until He was thirty years old. He was a carpenter by profession and it is mentioned that He always amazed His parents with spiritual insights, but aside from the incident of His remaining in the temple in Jerusalem amazing the teachers (Luke 2:40-52), we know nothing of His earlier years. He must have been a child obedient to His parents because He had to be without sin. When Jesus grew to manhood and started His public ministry, He understood His assignment.

God needed a perfect Lamb to die for the sins of the people. All of Israel knew about the importance of lambs and sacrifices because it had been instituted for years through Moses. People knew that the only way for atonement was through shed blood. The entire Old Testament foreshadowed the coming of the true Messiah who would take away the world's sins. Jesus, with His sinless Blood which came from the Father, was that Person. At the start of His ministry, we see Jesus laying down His carpentry tools and going into the wilderness where He saw John baptizing in the Jordan River. Upon seeing Jesus, John immediately received spiritual illumination (John 1:29): "The next day John seeth Jesus coming unto Him, and saith, Behold the Lamb of God, which taketh away the sin of the world,"

As soon as Jesus was baptized in water by John and the Spirit descended upon Him. the Spirit led Him into the wilderness to be tested. He had to be man to go through tests and learn obedience through the things He suffered. The enemy tempted Jesus as a man and it was entirely possible for Jesus to yield to temptation. Many people think Jesus was entirely supernatural in His role on earth, but He had all the attributes of a man. We can never look at Jesus and say, "He could accomplish certain things, but we cannot because of our humanity." The only difference between Jesus and other men was the unpolluted Blood in His body.

Jesus was often subjected to temptation by Satan to cause Him to depart from God's plan for His life. When He told His disciples He had to die, Peter vehemently opposed Him and said that such a thing should not happen. According to Matthew 16:23, He turned and said unto Peter, "Get thee behind me Satan: thou art an offense unto me: for thou savourest not the things that be of God, but those that be of men." Because Jesus never yielded to temptation, He could stand before the enemy at the end of His life and say, "Satan, you have nothing on Me." Fortunately Satan did not understand the entire revelation and mystery of the crucifixion, because he thought he had Jesus permanently when He died on the cross.

Jesus was fully aware that the seed of life was within His Blood. He knew the John 12:24 principle revealed to Adam: "Verily, verily, I say unto you, Except a corn of wheat fall into the ground and die, it abideth alone: but if it die, it bringeth forth much fruit." That is why scripture says Jesus endured the cross because of the joy that lay ahead. Just as Adam received his Eve by submitting to a deathlike state, so Jesus would receive His bride by enduring the cross. He knew that by His bloodshed we would be redeemed back to the Father, and we would be one with Him. Hebrews 12:2 affirms this: "Looking unto Jesus the author and finisher of our faith; who for the joy that was set before Him endured the cross, despising the shame, and is set down at the right hand of the throne of God." This is like a love song about what Jesus thinks of us. We are His Eve and He went to the cross for the joy of a relationship with us. And we question if God loves us?

Because God is love, He needs an object upon which to pour out His love, He created man so He would have someone to love and receive what He had to give. God can be holy and righteous by Himself, but cannot be love by Himself. Man was made to be a receiver of His love.

C. Heading to the Cross

The first time Scripture mentions the shedding of Blood from the body of Jesus is in the Garden of Gethsemane.

Luke, a physician and a disciple of Jesus, looked at the whole scene in the Garden through a doctor's eyes. When Jesus wept in the garden, He began to agonize in the spirit. Jesus the man had human emotions and did not want to go through suffering, but in His spirit He knew He had to fulfill God's plan of a sacrificed Lamb. We see in the Garden the conflict between His human body and His deified spirit. The spirit was saying, "For this cause I came into the world to shed my Blood for the sins of mankind." He was weak in His humanity, but strong in His deity.

> And he went a little further, and fell on His face, and prayed, saying, "O my Father, if it be possible, let this cup pass from me: nevertheless not as I will but as thou wilt. (Matthew 26:39)

Even at this point, Jesus Christ could have given up on God's plan; He was capable of sinning and had a will. But because He was a man who knew God and knew from whom to draw His strength, He was obedient. That is why you often read that Jesus spent the early morning in prayer talking to His Father. If He had sinned, His Blood would become just like Adam's blood.

The first time Jesus began to shed blood was in Luke 22:44: "And being in an agony He prayed more earnestly: and His sweat was as it were great drops of Blood falling down to the ground." There is a medical explanation for sweating blood. As Jesus underwent the stress and agony of being obedient His heart was racing and His nervous system was so traumatized with agony that His body went amok. Blood that usually flows through strong blood vessels took a different course. It flowed out of the vessels, through the subcutaneous layer of the skin, to the sweat glands, and came out of the body.

Immediately after His experience in the Garden, He was taken and lashed with the cat-of-nine tails. Inside of each tail of these reeds was an exposed blade. Nine blades were in each whip. Every time the soldier hit the back of Jesus, at least nine open sores came from one lash. This means 39 lashes times 9 blades brought 351 open bleeding sores.

D. The Work of the Cross

The scripture says that Christ was made to be sin for us, but He Himself never sinned. The sins of the world were placed on Him. Sin did not get into Him and His Blood remained pure. The act on the cross satisfied God's justice because sin had to be punished. God cannot stand in the presence of sin. The willingness of Jesus to go to the cross and take on every sin a person did or ever will do satisfied God's justice. Because one died for all sins, there is no need for anyone else to die for sins. When Jesus gave His life, we were freed from the second death. His death brought newness of life to us. This is God's mercy that gives us something we do not deserve. Jesus's shed Blood immediately provided the vehicle for a spiritual transfusion.

Jesus knew His death would reestablish the life-giving Blood of the Father into the earth again. There was a joy in redeeming man back to right standing with God. All man had to do now was receive the Blood of Jesus in order to be like the first Adam. Jesus was called the second Adam because He gained back the standing with God that the first Adam had lost. The second Adam had become what the first Adam was created to be.

When Jesus shed His Blood, He did not just cover you. He took away every sin you ever had and cast it into the sea of forgetfulness. When you come to Him, you are freed from the guilt of sin.

> For if the blood of bulls and of goats, and the ashes of an heifer sprinkling the unclean, sanctifieth to the purifying of the flesh: How much more shall the Blood of Christ, who through the eternal Spirit offered Himself without spot to God, purge your conscience from dead works to serve the living God? (Hebrews 9-13-14).

The Blood has universality to it. It is a cleansing agent, power agent, healing agent and life-giving agent. When the Blood began to flow—first in the Garden of Gethsemane, then from the thirty-nine lashes He received for our healing, and from the crown of thorns placed on His head on the cross, and then from the nails being driven into His hands and feet—every drop of Blood was bringing something into the world that had not been there before. This Blood brought us redemption, reconciliation, healing, justification, power, and forgiveness. It covered every need mankind ever had.

Amid the two robbers on crosses, Jesus was the first to die. His legs were not broken as with the other men. Breaking legs during crucifixion caused a person to die quicker because the victim could no longer push himself up with his feet to gasp for air. The psalmist had already prophesied that: "He keepeth all His bones: not one of them is broken." Man did not take Jesus life, He instead "gave up the ghost"—gave up His life—and at that point His work on the cross was finished. Just as His body was crucified on the cross, all the sin of the world and all the rules and ordinances of the world were pinned to the cross. Jesus was made to be sin for us.

E. Journey Into Hell

Upon His death, Jesus went to hell for three days and nights: "Now that He ascended, what is it but that He also descended first into the lower parts of the earth?" (Ephesians 4:9). He entered hell legally because He died because of sin; without sin there can be no death. Jesus had no sin but was made to be sin for us. Satan and his demons in hell were probably having a party thinking they had the Son of God in their grasp. I can hear them taunting: "We have you now, Jesus—you are ours. What are you going to do now?" Suddenly the Resurrection Power came forth and the incorruptible Blood which was full of life and light began its work. Jesus, blinding the inhabitants of the kingdom of darkness rose up and grabbed the keys of death and hell from Satan. He freed all the people who were waiting for a redeemer and gave us new life—rebirth had come! The triumph for eternity can be seen in Revelation 1:18: "I am He that liveth and was dead; and, behold, I am alive forevermore, Amen; and have the keys of hell and of death." Jesus took the keys and spoiled principalities and powers.

F. Blood Still Alive

Unlike our blood, which decomposes at the point of death, the Blood of Jesus lives on. I Peter 1:23 says, "Being born again, not of corruptible seed, but of incorruptible, by the Word of God, which liveth and abideth for ever." The Blood of Jesus lives on in the throne room of the heavenly tabernacle and is sprinkled on the mercy seat. His Blood still speaks today and says, "Mercy, mercy to you."

Every time the enemy wants to accuse you and point out your past mistakes, we can allow the Blood to speak for us. It says, "Mercy over your misdeeds and mistakes." Time and again scriptures say we are washed by the Blood of the Lamb. To God, sins are not even visible anymore and the enemy has nothing on you. Look at the Apostle Paul who wreaked havoc among Christians before he became a Christian. After his conversion, he freely said, "I have done no wrong. The shedding of Jesus' Blood remits my sins and I forget the things of my past." That is why scripture says, "If we confess our sins, he is faithful and just to forgive us our sins and to cleanse us from all unrighteousness." (I John 1:9) There is no condemnation from God once a person has repented. Repentance means a person turns around and does not repeat the offense again and again. Some people are only sorry when they are caught doing wrong; a repentant person is remorseful regardless and does not intend to repeat the offense.

G. Lamb Slain

Many names have been given to Jesus to refer to His character, including the "Lion of the tribe of Judah." But when it comes to the sacrificial work on the cross, He is referred to as the Lamb. Why was Jesus described as a lamb? Jesus exemplified all the characteristics of lambs—humble, gentle, innocent, and pure. His meekness even in the face of death is seen in Isaiah 53:7, "He was oppressed, and He was afflicted, yet He opened not His mouth." Jesus had no sin when He went to the cross, but allowed sin to be placed on Him so He could enter hell in our place.

After reading a story about men who were slaughtering a lamb and a pig, I learned that lambs will go to slaughter without a fight. Pigs will fight and squeal until they die—they fight off death until the end. But a lamb will be strung up and in resignation allow its blood to drain out. Jesus went to the cross as a lamb. He did not cry out or give a fierce fight. He did not have to be violent to redeem us. No one took His life; He gave it freely.

The phrase "washed in the Blood of the Lamb" has a beautiful significance. In the sheep herding business, a mother ewe who gives birth to a dead baby, or whose baby dies, refuses to allow another lamb to suckle from her. She does not want to feed a lamb that is not her own. But when the shepherd needs to use the milk from that ewe to feed an orphaned lamb, he can fool the ewe into thinking the orphaned lamb belongs to her. He takes the blood from the dead lamb and washes the orphaned lamb in the blood. When the mother ewe who lost the baby sniffs the lamb, it smells like her own and she takes that lamb to nurture it. This is similar to what Jesus did for us by His Blood. We were adopted into His family and made joint heirs with Him by His Blood. We were transformed from servants into sons and can lean on the Father's breast and receive life.

Jesus Christ is also called the Lamb slain from the foundation of the world in Revelation 13:8, and not the Lamb slain at the end of the world. "And all that dwell upon the earth shall worship Him, whose names are not written in the book of life of the Lamb slain from the foundation of the world." Note that the work of the cross was already planned and accomplished in God's eternal "time frame," even before man sinned. Jesus, the man, entered into our time and walked out what was already done in God's mind. It goes beyond my imagination that Christ would leave the splendor of heaven and its honor to come to earth and lay down His life. It is hard to fathom that He would go to the cross, take on the sin of the world, and experience the pain of crucifixion out of His love for us.

H. Types of the Perfect Lamb

The importance of a lamb and the need to sacrifice lambs is seen in seven different Old Testament examples. The perfect lambs required for sacrifice in the Old Testament were only shadows and foretypes of Jesus Christ who would be the perfect sacrificial Lamb without spot or blemish.

The first sacrifice for sin was in the Garden of Eden, when God clothed Adam and Eve with a skin. To get an animal's skin, you have to shed blood. Man is learning from the beginning of creation the necessity of a covering for sin through the shedding of blood. Throughout the Old Testament, lambs were sacrificed and their blood presented in the holy of holies. Whenever the priest and people sacrificed a lamb, they were not allowed to eat the blood. The reason they couldn't eat it was because God was giving them an appreciation of the life in the blood. That is why laws were set up in the Old Testament that said, "If you kill a man and shed his blood, you will be killed." Man was to have an appreciation for life.

The second sacrificial lamb was in the story of Cain and Abel. Abel was a sheepherder and Cain was a farmer. God knew the attitude of their hearts when it came time for a sacrifice, Abel knew that without the shedding of blood you cannot satisfy God. Cain knew it as well because it had been taught to him by his father, but he had a haughty attitude and brought the fruit of his field instead. That was unacceptable and he knew it, but he wanted to do things his way. God rejected his gift on the basis of his attitude as well as the gift itself.

The third sacrificial lamb is seen in the story of Abraham and Isaac. Abraham knew he must obey God at any cost. He knew to trust God when He said to sacrifice his only son, who God had given him. God was using Abraham as a foretype so we would understand what it was like to give up an only son as God would later do with Jesus, except with Abraham God stopped him at the point at which he was about to sacrifice his son and provided a substitute animal.

> And he said, Lay not thine hand upon the lad, neither do thou any thing unto him: for now I know that thou fearest God, seeing thou has not withheld thy son, thine only son from me. And Abraham lifted up his eyes, and looked, and behold behind him a ram caught in a thicket by his horns: and Abraham went and took the ram, and offered him up for a burnt offering in the stead of his son. (Genesis 22:12-13)

Let us look deeper into the relationship between God and Abraham. Abraham had a blood covenant with God. This is a popular ritual in Far

Eastern countries. When two people established a blood covenant, they were true to one another as long as they lived. Whatever belonged to one belonged to the other. One person would always stand up for the other. These covenants were entered into with the shedding of blood.

God established with Abraham the circumcision of male children as a way to shed blood down through the generations. God could have required circumcision on any part of the body, but He chose the organ of procreation so every time it was used to procreate, the male would remember he had a covenant with God—a life-giving covenant. Abraham's side of the bargain was to shed blood by circumcision, although God would not be ready to fulfill his part of the covenant until Jesus died on the cross.

When Jesus came and was circumcised, that was not yet the completion of the covenant. Jesus was relating to mankind and saying, "Through me you will be heirs to Abraham. If I am not an heir of Abraham, then you cannot be an heir of Abraham; therefore, I will be circumcised too." Although circumcision began to fulfill His covenant relationship with Abraham, the complete covenant with mankind was to shed blood in death. It was not enough for Him just to be wounded, Jesus had to die.

To help to understand why Jesus had to die, let me relate this example. In old times when leprosy was rampant, there was no cure for the death organism in the leper's blood. In old medical history, they found the way to cure a leper was to get rid of his old blood and bring in new blood. The leper needed a transfusion, and in order for him to receive healing, someone had to give his life. I do not know if they even had a system for keeping blood in those times because if it is not stored correctly it corrupts once it leaves the body. It took the entire blood of a man to cleanse a leper. As the new blood flowed into him, life flowed out of the donor. Can you envision the blood flowing into the leper? One heart pumping life into the body of another until the donor's life ebbed away. Can you see that same act in Jesus? It was not just His death that gave us life. It was his Blood going into us that made us clean as the leper was made clean. In death He gave all His Blood, that we might have life and that we might be cleansed. The Blood of Jesus constantly cleanses us. How precious is the scripture:

> And from Jesus Christ, who is the faithful witness, and the first begotten of the dead, and the prince of the kings of the earth. Unto Him that loved us, and washed us from our sins in His own Blood, and hath made us kings and priests unto God and His Father; to Him be glory and dominion for ever and ever. Amen. (Revelation 1:5-6)

In the fourth example, God revealed the importance of the slain lamb and the coming Messiah through the Passover lamb. Every family was to take a male lamb without blemish out of the flock and place the blood in a basin. Then they were to take hyssop and dip it in blood in order to preserve the life of their firstborn sons. Before the sun went down, they would keep their families inside the house and apply the blood over their door post. As long as the death angel saw the protective blood, He passed over and the lives of the firstborn sons were saved. In the same way, God passes over our sins when He sees us covered by the Blood of Jesus.

Although we will explore in depth the significance of the Blood and water that poured out of Jesus's side when it was pierced on the cross, these significant symbols of blood and water are seen in the Old Testament. The hyssop was a watery plant that was dipped in blood and then sprinkled. God is foreshadowing even then how He would lay down His life as the perfect Lamb in order to give new life.

The fifth lamb we see in the Old Testament is the scapegoat sent into the wilderness. Two lambs were taken from the same herd. One was to shed blood and the other was a sin-bearing animal. Hands were laid on the scape-goat as a symbol of all the sins of Israel. This animal was to bear all the sins of the colony and then to be released into the wilderness where the sins could not be seen or remembered anymore. This was a foretype of Jesus who was our sacrifice and scapegoat. He took our sins to the cross so they would be forgotten.

The sixth lamb was foreshadowed by the prophet Isaiah as the suffering Lamb of God. This Lamb is described as the fulfillment of all God's prom-ises when divine incorruptible Blood would transfuse man's blood and restore him from the fall.

> Surely he hath borne our griefs, and carried our sorrows; yet we did esteem him stricken, smitten of God, and afflict-ed. But he was wounded for our transgressions, he was bruised for our iniquities: the chastisement of our peace was upon him; and with His stripes we are healed. All we like sheep have gone astray; we have turned every one to his own way; and the Lord hath laid on Him the iniquity of us all. He was oppressed, and He was afflicted, yet He opened not His mouth. (Isaiah 53:4-7)

The difference between lambs and other animals is how they accept death. Jesus displayed the property of a lamb when He did not run from death. He was the seventh Lamb. He knew the John 12:24 principle we have discussed: "Verily, verily, I say unto you. Except a corn of wheat fall into the ground and die, it abideth alone: but if it die, it bringeth forth much fruit." Jesus knew He had to lay down His life to bear fruit. That is why God called Him the Lamb.

Many shepherds in Israel kept flocks of sheep and understood the ways of sheep and sheep herding. They understood the animal's dependency upon the shepherd and the fact that their undisciplined natures had to be trained. God often referred to His people as sheep. God wanted us to see

Jesus as a Lamb among the sheep. He even said He came to save the lost sheep of Israel who were strays. The shepherd utilizes a specific method in his sheep herding to bring back stray sheep. He takes a pet lamb who is trained to obey and love and puts it among the stray sheep. Then when he calls the lamb, the other sheep follow him. How beautiful to realize that Jesus is like that pet lamb that brings in stray sheep.

Chapter Five

Using the Weaponry of Blood

Jesus literally gave His life in order to receive life for you. Jesus did not die in vain, but completed the work on the cross to provide you with all the weapons you would need to live a successful life. The work of His Blood in the spiritual realm allows you to be adopted into His family and reign with Jesus. You are a son instead of a servant and can lean on your Heavenly Father and receive His life.

The spiritual transfusion you have received enables you to be reconnected to God and is your tool to utilize because the Blood of Jesus has not lost its power. We have to realize that the Blood of Jesus is a multifaceted and unique end-time weapon in the line of defense against the enemy. Let us examine the areas in which God wants you to utilize the Blood of Jesus in your life.

A. Eternal Life

When Jesus shed His Blood, He did not just cover you, He cleansed you by taking away your sins and casting them into the sea of forgetfulness. When He forgives you, your past sins are no longer visible and Satan has nothing to hold over you. According to II Corinthians 5:17, "Therefore if any man be in Christ, he is a new creature: old things are passed away; behold, all things are become new."

Once you accept Jesus Christ into your life, you are to be God's receiver. You have been made like Him by His Spirit so you can receive His love and fellowship with Him. Your body becomes a house for Christ. Unlike the people in the Old Testament who could not enjoy the benefits of being born-again, the death and resurrection of Jesus brought you into relationship with the Father God.

Ephesians 1:5 tells us it was the will of the Father to bring us into His family: "Having predestinated us unto the adoption of children by Jesus Christ to Himself, according to the good pleasure of His will..," but He had to use the Blood of Jesus as the vehicle to cleanse us before He could redeem us. Jesus went to the cross to redeem you because you are the object of His love, but you must have a revelation of the love of God and be in love with the Giver. If you love somebody, you will have faith in that person.

Faith works by love according to Galatians 5:6. You have to understand God loves you before you can receive and have faith in God.

Now that we have studied that Jesus was the vehicle for God to transfuse our blood and eliminate the polluted blood passed on by Adam, we realize that eternal life is only given by accepting the fact that Jesus died and shed His Blood for us. His precious Blood, which cannot corrupt or decay, was sprinkled on the mercy seat in heaven's tabernacle where it constantly pleads your case before the Father. "Neither by the blood of goats and calves, but by his own Blood He entered in once into the holy place, having obtained eternal redemption for us." (Hebrews 9:12).

The Blood on the mercy seat of heaven speaks for you. It says, "Lord, they are forgiven and Satan no longer has a case against them." Jesus the lawyer is saying to Satan, "You are out of order so throw that case out. My Blood has wiped their slate clean." But when the enemy comes to accuse you, you must choose to believe the report of the Blood of Jesus over the accusations of the enemy.

When Jesus died, we were crucified, buried, and resurrected in power with Him. The same Spirit that raised Jesus from the dead raised us and dwells in us. Through this identification with the work of Christ on the cross, we can begin to realize the provision given to us. Ephesians 1:3-4 tells us, "Blessed be the God and Father of our Lord Jesus Christ, who has blessed us with all spiritual blessings in heavenly places in Christ: According as He hath chosen us in Him before the foundation of the world, that we should be holy and without blame before Him in love." We are given ALL spiritual blessings.

In giving His life and shedding His Blood, Jesus knew He was going to bring forth life in you and would have you as His counterpart to carry out His work. This is the mystery of the Gospel that the man Jesus could lay down His life and consequently produce more life. If Satan understood this multiplication effect, He would never have planned to kill Jesus. Every time a person comes into God's kingdom, another piece of the puzzle is put in place, and each new Christian further enhances the Body of Christ. You have the ability to overcome the enemy once you become a Christian. "Who is he that overcometh the world, but he that believeth that Jesus is the Son of God?" (I John 5:5).

B. Cleansing

In the Old Testament, God lived in or manifested His presence in tabernacles made with men's hands. The tabernacles of God today are our bodies. God bought them with His Blood so He can live in them, because God needs a body to manifest Himself on earth. It is an ongoing battle for the Christian determining who rules his body. You are either inhabited by the Spirit of God or the spirit of darkness, which is Satan. The two cannot dwell in the same place. When darkness is in you, the light is gone. If light is present, it will overpower the darkness. When Adam sinned, God could not communicate with Him any longer because he allowed darkness to enter by eating the fruit. Darkness is the absence of light, not the destruction of light; Adam's lights went out because he allowed darkness to enter. As Christians today, we cannot worship other gods like the children of Israel who insisted on a golden calf to worship. How can we worship other gods when we realize God has provided His own Son? We are people called by His Name. If we choose to wear the name of Christian and call ourselves by the name of Christ, we need to live holy before Him. We cannot come into His presence with sin.

Romans 12:2 says, "And be not conformed to this world: but be ye transformed by the renewing of your mind, that ye may prove what is that good, and acceptable, and perfect will of God." It is not difficult to be holy because Jesus made us holy by His Blood. If we keep our eyes on Jesus and hear what the Spirit of God is saying to His church, we would get rid of the gods in our lives. These gods or idols can be in the form of money, position, family relationships, or even worshipping our children. We cannot let the world determine who is God because you will be deceived if you keep one eye on the world and one eye on Jesus. You will find yourself compromising who is on the throne of your life.

I have great joy in my life because I invite Jesus to keep changing me. Every day I ask the Lord to search my heart and see if any wicked way is in me, and every day God has to clean me up. I ask Him to cleanse me so I can be a vessel of honor. Just as an earthly father disciplines his child out of love, we need the discipline of the Heavenly Father. When God shows us something to change in our life, it is because He loves us.

God needs us in the kingdom and wants to use us, but He will never make robots out of us. God can do whatever He wills, but He will never override man's free will. That is why Adam paid a huge consequence with his wrong choice. God told him, "If you obey Me, you will continue to have my spiritual life. If you don't obey Me, you will have spiritual death." Adam and Eve obeyed Satan instead of God and took on the nature of their new god. Their Godlike blood was contaminated because the alien substance named sin entered in.

The devil poses the same question to Christians today as he did to Adam and Eve. "Did God really say that to you?" You may be believing for something God promised you, and the enemy will come in some form and say, "Did God really say that?" When we give into his thoughts, we begin our demise.

The first time the children of Israel did wrong, they did not completely fall. But in the fullness of time, judgment worked out in their lives. Adam's sin did not bring immediate death, but the death process began to work out in his life. Christians cannot continue to go against the Word of God and live halfway between the kingdom of God and the kingdom of darkness.

You can play church and fool other people, but God knows if there is sin in your life. When you ask God to search your heart, He will search out sin. The only reason we are not living in death is because of the Blood of Jesus. This fact brings with it a responsibility to walk in holiness. Leviticus 11:45 says, "For I am the Lord that bringeth you up out of the land of Egypt, to be your God: ye shall therefore be holy, for I am holy,"

Many false doctrines are trying to enter the church today and Christians cannot stand against them without a knowledge of the Word. Satan doesn't come in with doctrines altogether different than the Bible, he comes with something that sounds like the real thing. That is why God says to keep His Word before you day and night. Never get to the place where you think you know it all, because God by His Spirit continues to teach you.

C. Protection

When the children of Israel needed to cross the Red Sea, a mighty wind came and lifted up the water. The water served as walls on each side of them while God's people walked through on dry land. The Red Sea experience once again exemplifies the symbolism of water and blood. The Red Sea, which typifies the blood, is what gave them their life, but the same blood that gave them life became death to their enemies. As the walls of water went up and protected them, the walls came down on the enemies when Moses stretched our his hand over the waters. Even today, the blood that gives us life is the Blood of Jesus spoken over our enemy, and that Blood will cause his destruction.

Throughout scripture water and blood are utilized. We need to learn how to apply the Blood like the Israelites did. The principle of salvation found in Romans 10:9 can be utilized in applying the Blood. "That if thou shalt confess with thy mouth the Lord Jesus, and shalt believe in thine heart that God hath raised him from the dead, thou shalt be saved." In salvation, you believe in your heart and speak that belief out of your mouth and receive eternal life. It is the same with the Blood. As you believe in your heart what the Blood has done for you and speak it out of your mouth, you are protected. The same Blood that gives you eternal life is the Blood that keeps you from the enemy. The same Blood that gives you life brings death to your enemy. The Red Sea symbolized that unique combination of blood and water—giving life to the Israelites and death to the enemy.

The enemy knows if you really understand who you are in Jesus Christ and whether you have a revelation that Jesus died for you. The enemy cannot do anything against you once you realize the power in the Blood of Jesus; it is a repellent to him. When you put the Blood around you, the enemy is virtually paralyzed. You cannot apply the Blood physically, but in the spiritual realm you apply it and then plug up the cracks in the hedge of protection. Everything you need in this life is found in Jesus' Blood. If you are not obedient to apply the Blood, it will not work for you. Once you apply the Blood, keep on standing and do not allow sin to enter in. Revelation 12:11 says, "And they overcame him by the Blood of the Lamb, and by the word of their testimony; and they loved not their lives unto the death." If you are not testifying on what you have in Jesus Christ, you will not win the battle.

D. Healing

I Peter 2:24 is instrumental in understanding the healing provided to us through the Blood of Jesus. "Who His own self bare our sins in His own body on the tree, that we, being dead to sins should live unto righteousness: by whose stripes ye were healed." The anointing for healing is still present in the church today. The same Blood shed that redeemed you from sin will heal you. The stripes Jesus took on His back referred to a cat of nine tails instrument used in beatings. He took thirty-nine lashes with razor-sharp knives in the end of each of the nine cat tails. Every lash brought nine open wounds as 351 wounds were inflicted on the body of Jesus. As the Blood began to ooze out, the life-giving healing blood began to spill on the earth. These stripes healed you even before full redemption came from the cross. Jesus bled for healing before He went to the cross and bled for sins.

Whenever something is good, Satan tries to make a mockery of it. The most powerful thing available is the Blood of Jesus. Therefore, the enemy has come in the most destructive way to destroy it. Satan works against God's Blood as he invades the earthly realm with the disease of AIDS that degenerates the entire body. Many scientists agree that AIDS is comparable to the bubonic plague of the past. One of the first doctors to diagnose an AIDS case agreed, "You cannot conceive of a disease that is more disruptive and disturbing than AIDS. It could prove to be the plague of the millennium."

AIDS works in three stages. The first stage is asymptotic where people carry the virus, but symptoms do not manifest even though others can be infected. It is like a dangerous iceberg hidden under the water. The second stage is AIDS-related complex. The virus is not full-blown although some symptoms related to AIDS may emerge. It can take from two to thirty years to enter the third, full-blown stage. We do not see AIDS for a long time because it is a virus that slowly manifests itself. It cannot be detected because it keeps on changing its form. It is so deceptive that it can exist in the body for years without anyone's knowledge. The virus enters into the body hidden in a cell from another person's blood or bodily secretion. Once it is inside your body, it begins to affect the cells. It is so deceptive that the body's t-cell, the purpose of which is to destroy enemy invaders, cannot go and tell the other cells to fight it. As soon as the AIDS virus comes in contact with the t-cell whose purpose was to destroy the enemy, it gets inside the t-cell and disables it. With the blood's mainline man disabled and unable to tell others what is coming, the virus gradually destroys the body's immune system.

We have what we need in the Blood of Jesus to come against AIDS. When those wounds opened up on Jesus' back, God released the life-giving power bottled up in Jesus to spill on the earth. No wonder the devil lies and says healing is not for today! Never let anyone tell you healing is not for today because He shed His Blood for healing before He went to the cross to redeem you.

Jesus died, but His incorruptible Blood was alive. I Peter 1:18-19 describes your purchase, "Forasmuch as ye know that ye were not redeemed with corruptible things, as silver and gold, from your vain conversation received by tradition from your fathers; but with the precious Blood of Christ, as of a lamb without blemish and without spot."

You have to realize God wants life for you and those dying around you. I remember going to visit a dying young woman in a coma with sickle cell anemia. The only thing that could help her was prayer and the Word of God used in faith. An illumination came into my spirit that the scripture regarding polluted blood applied to her. Believing she could hear me in her comatose state, I began to read the Word to her and knew it was going into her spirit. I read the scripture from Ezekiel 16:6, "And when I passed by thee, and saw thee polluted in thine own blood, I said unto thee when thou wast in thy blood, Live; yea, I said unto thee when thou wast in thy blood, Live." About a month later, she came out of the hospital. Her polluted blood had been cleansed by the Word of God.

E. Power or Authority

The person who does not understand why the Blood of Jesus is so powerful in his life will never be free from the enemy. The enemy can attack and attach himself to Christians. Oppressive spirits can come in the form of condemnation, oppression, obsession, or depression, but the first road to deliverance from oppression is identifying that God wants you free. If you don't believe His shed Blood gives you authority, you will never stand, take your rightful place, and cancel the enemy's assignment against you.

We are commanded in Galatians 5:1 to, "Stand fast therefore in the liberty wherewith Christ hath made us free, and be not entangled again with the yoke of bondage." Jesus said He gave all power on earth to us by accomplishing His finished work on the cross, but we have to call on His Name and authority in the power of the Blood and believe that no weapon formed against us will prosper. Do not allow the enemy to dominate anything you believe in the Word of God because God is in your midst. When David saw the giant Philistine named Goliath who was intimidating the army of God, he was defiant against him. His retort to the enemy of God was:

> Then said David to the Philistine, Thou comest to me with a sword, and with a spear, and with a shield: but I come to thee in the Name of the Lord of hosts, the God of the armies of Israel, whom thou has defied. This day will the Lord deliver thee into mine hand; and I will smite thee, and

take thine head from thee; and I will give the carcasses of the host of the Philistines this day unto the fowls of the air, and to the wild beasts of the earth; that all the earth may know that there is a God in Israel. And all this assembly shall know that the Lord saveth not with sword and spear: for the battle is the Lord's, and he will give you into our hands. (I Samuel 17:45-47).

God is in the midst of every battle we fight. You are not alone or left defenseless. Remember Revelation 12:11 which says, "And they overcame him by the Blood of the Lamb, and by the word of their testimony; and they loved not their lives unto the death." Just show the devil your belief in the Blood of Jesus and speak out how your life, family, and circumstances are covered by this Blood. The Blood is your nuclear weapon in the end times. God's people need to stand up and endure to the end because the enemy is looking for people to destroy. We cannot give in and cringe because we think the devil is strong. He hasn't got the degree of power that has been given to you by Jesus. Say to Satan, "The Blood of Jesus covers me and you have to move back," and he will. You have to constantly meditate in God's Word and let it dwell mightily in you.

We cannot weary of Satan or fear what he might do. You have authority given to you by Jesus. Being married to Jesus has similar privileges to being married to an earthly husband. A woman has the authority to use her earthly husband's name and stand in his place. You can use his charge cards and make withdrawals at the bank. Most wives will not stand back and say, "I don't have the authority to use the money to buy groceries or clothes," yet many times we stand back even though God has given us all the power and authority to use His name. I want Jesus to be proud of me as His bride. I do not want my privileges to go unused. When certain things belong to me, I often have to go through a legal battle with the devil, who creates opposition to try to prove to me that I am not victorious. The negative thoughts that come are not from God. They are thoughts from the devil that exalt themselves above the Word of God.

As I bathe in the Word and realize I am married to Jesus Christ, I am not lacking anything. We cannot be deceived, fall asleep, and let the enemy run roughshod over us simply because we do not know the power given to us. Learn about the power in the Blood because the enemy cannot stand against the Blood. Be armed with the Word of God and the Blood and Satan is paralyzed. You are strong in Christ and the power of His might.

F. Freedom from Religion and Laws

No laws made by men can get us into salvation. The scriptures clearly point out that we are all prisoners of sin, and faith in Jesus Christ is the only way of escape.

> But the scripture hath concluded all under sin, that the
> promise by faith of Jesus Christ might be given to them
> that believe. But before faith came, we were kept under the
> law, shut up unto the faith which should afterwards be
> revealed Wherefore the law was our schoolmaster to bring
> us unto Christ, that we might be justified by faith.
> (Galatians 3:22-24).

The Jewish laws were the teachers and guides until Christ came and gave right standing with God through faith. We do not need to be in bondage under the elements of this world now that Christ has come; He redeemed us from the curse of the law. He did not come to scratch out the laws, but to fulfill them in Himself. Jesus is now our law unto salvation. No person can obey the law in their own strength; if a person could, he would not need a redeemer. However, God knew our human weakness and inability to meet the requirements of the law so He gave us Jesus Christ and His shed Blood.

Scripture often refers to the precious Blood of Jesus. It is precious because it gives us freedom from the many things that bind us. The Blood gives us freedom from bondage. That does not mean we are given a license to go out and do whatever we want, it means He died so we could be free from rules, ordinances, and regulation—the law. The only law we have to fulfill in our lives now is found in Matthew 22:37-39:

> Jesus said unto him, Thou shalt love the Lord thy God with
> all thy heart, and with all thy soul, and with all thy mind.
> This is the first and great commandment. And the second is
> like unto it, Thou shalt love thy neighbor as thyself.

If we can fulfill loving God and loving our neighbors, there is no need for other commandments. There is quietness and confidence in knowing that we do not have to strive in the natural realm to obey constant rules and ordinances to please God. All He wants us to do is love Him. Jesus Himself introduced agape love. This love was much deeper than the mankind type of love.

God's nature and character is made up of love. God is a loving Father who has chosen and drawn you to Himself even before the foundation of the world. His every action is rooted in love, but His love still needs to be reciprocated. God wants a people who will receive His unconditional love and then love Him back unconditionally. He does not want your love just because He does something for you or guides you in the way you want to be guided. We are to love God with all your heart, soul, mind, and strength. When we do this, we will move into being delighted with the Lord. According to Psalm 37:4, "Delight thyself also in the Lord: and He shall give thee the desires of thine heart."

When we spend time in His presence, we get to know Him by the Spirit. As we do this, we become open channels to receive His Word when He speaks. When we delight in Him, He is able to fill us with His desires according to His Word. As we concentrate on Jesus and spend time in His Word, His desires become our desires and He fulfills them.

Chapter Six

Walking in Light and Life

I remember standing by the Sea of Galilee when I traveled to Israel. As soon as night came, lights from the cities were sprinkled across the hillsides. The cities could not be hid because their lights would shine across the Galilean Sea.

Just like cities in the night, Christians have this effect in the world of darkness as long as they keep their light turned on. Jesus gave us His life and light, but are we allowing that light to shine? Satan wants to make a mockery of our temples and dim the light in our tabernacles. Yet every time we plead the Blood of Jesus we are turning on our light and sending the enemy fleeing in terror.

A. The Nature of Light

We need a revelation of Matthew 6:22 and 23 to understand the importance of keeping our light bright:

> The light of the body is the eye: if therefore thine eye be single, thy whole body shall be full of light. But if thine eye be evil, thy whole body shall be full of darkness. If therefore the light that is in thee be darkness, how great is that darkness!

We realize that light and darkness are opposites. So what does the scripture imply when it refers to the light in a person being darkness? There is counterfeit light which is a deception of the enemy. The scripture says the devil can appear as an angel of light. Deceptive lights are what the enemy pulls out to deceive us.

There are people who are not really lights of the truth. If you allow the light of their doctrines to enter in, you receive all different rays of light. Wrong doctrines appear as vehicles of light, but they are not light. They come from many different places. You receive the evil reports of the world and your eye is not single because the single truth of Jesus Christ who is the Way, Truth, and the Life (light) is not within you. The only single light is the light of God in Jesus Christ. Receiving other pseudo-lights brings darkness and eventually death. That is why you have to receive the true light. Other lights may form a spectrum composed of different beams, rays, and colors. White light is a single light. The true light, Jesus Christ, is a single light.

B. Laser Light

Laser light is the only light that has a strong single beam of one color that can strengthen other lights. Laser is an acronym for light amplified stimulated emission of radiation, which means light is amplified in increasing strength by causing something to give off more light. This means laser increases the strength of another light by causing it to give off more light. All matter is made up of atoms which increase their energy level when excited. They do this by absorbing more energy.

The more excited the atoms, the faster they travel. A laser light causes electron activity and excites these small particles to move faster and put out more energy. The energy put out is in the form of light. This laser which is a light stimulator causes excited electrons to produce more energy and produce more light. These other lights will begin to move in the direction of the main laser light and in a sense become a reproduction of the main laser light. When they combine with the laser light, they have a single beam that goes in the same direction.

In the spiritual realm we see Jesus, the powerful light that strengthens other lights (members of the body of Christ), by stimulating or triggering them to give off more light. We are creatures of light, the kind of light that can get excited. Jesus excites and challenges us to give off more light. Jesus is our Laser Light who is strong and has a single path. He declared Himself to be the Light of the world. Jesus has His light in us and when He continually shines His light in our heart, He is energizing our light-producing ability.

As He strengthens us and causes us to become one with Him, we join together as a strong single beam and produce more light. We become just like Him when we allow Him to keep strengthening us with His laser beam. When we stand before the enemy speaking the Blood of Jesus and walking in His light, he cannot tell the difference between us and Jesus.

Through the Blood of Jesus, we have power in laser capacity. We can let our light shine because Jesus paid the whole price for the light to remain on. Laser surgery is used in hospitals to actually burn off what should not be in a person's body. It is so powerful that the doctor has to wear glasses to shield his eyes. If this laser is directed in the right place, it will burn right through a growth. Just as laser beams are used in the medical realm to burn off cataracts or tumors, the light in us is sharp. It gets rid of the dross when our eye is single on Him. When the light comes in, it is a purifier and sin remover. God can separate spirit from flesh with His laser beam. That is what God wants to be to His people—a laser beam that stimulates, strengthens, and burns up the chaff in their lives.

C. Light's Entrance Into the World

Let us look at the connection between the creation of light in Genesis and the true Light that came into the world. In Genesis 1:3-4, "And God said, Let there be light: and there was light. And God saw the light, that it was good; and God divided the light from the darkness." Obviously God did not put light on earth so all darkness would be dispelled. He had a time for light and a time for darkness.

Although earth is somewhat modeled after heaven, there is no night or darkness in heaven. The city of heaven is lit because of the life of the Lamb of God. Light reigns supreme in heaven, but on earth God is doing things in stages. He did not take all the darkness away from the earth, He just divided it into day and night and said light is good. Let us look at a scripture which tells us about the true Light. Take note of John 1:6-12.

> There was a man sent from God, whose name was John. The same came for a witness, to bear witness of the Light, that all men through Him might believe. He was not that Light, but was sent to bear witness of that Light. That was the true Light, which lighteth every man that cometh into the world. He was in the world, and the world was made by Him, and the world knew Him not. He came unto His own, and His own received Him not. But as many as received Him, to them gave He power to become the sons of God, even to them that believe on His Name.

Many people in that time thought John the Baptist was the Light, but he was only a witness of the true Light that could light every man that comes into the world. According to this scripture, every person has the possibility of being lit. It is like when people build a home and put in electrical lines. The home has all the potential to enjoy light because of the installed wires and lines. But if they are not connected to the source of power, there will be no light.

Through Jesus Christ, God has given every man the potential to have eternal life. He has the right electrical wires but needs the connection that comes through Jesus Christ. Faith makes it possible to believe God. According to John 1:12, the only ones given the power to become the sons of God were those who believed in Him. Their belief turned on the lights. If men do not believe, they cannot walk in the power of that light.

D. Equality of Life and Light

John 1:1-4 reveals the parallel between life and light.

> In the beginning was the Word, and the Word was with
> God, and the Word was God. The same was in the begin-
> ning with God. All things were made by Him; and without
> Him was not any thing made that was made. In Him was
> life; and the life was the light of men.

John, who wrote these scriptures, walked with Jesus as his best friend. He is writing what he knew about Jesus. When he says: "In Him was life; and the LIFE WAS THE LIGHT of men," he is saying that light is equal to life. In mathematics, it is possible to write equations and substitute one thing for another when two things are equal. What you substitute has the same meaning as what you replaced. If life and light are equal, then we can substitute them for each other. Let us take this equation back to the book of Genesis. "And the Lord God formed man of the dust of the ground, and breathed into his nostrils the breath of Life; and man became a living soul." (Genesis 2:7) Could we not say that God breathed into man the breath of Light since life equals light? So we see not only life in man's spirit, but also light.

We can also substitute our new equality in the principle of the Life of the flesh in the blood (Leviticus 17:11) and say that the Light of the flesh is in the blood. When God created man, he had life or light in his spiritual blood system. Adam had God's own breath of life (light) in him. He was so full of light that he was crowned or clothed with the glory of God. Psalm 8:4-5 says:

> What is man, that thou art mindful of him? and the son of
> man, that thou visitest him: For thou hast made him a lit-
> tle lower than the angels, and hast crowned him with glory
> and honour.

Adam was the first person to have God's pure light in Him until the coming of Jesus.

When Adam was given the responsibility to guard the garden, he was guarding against darkness. We now know that Satan is the prince of darkness and when Adam and Eve listened to him, he became their master. The Light could not stand to be in the presence of darkness. Darkness cannot put out light but the two cannot occupy the same place at the same time. Therefore, God could no longer have fellowship with man because He could not reside in the same place as darkness, and by Adam's act of disobedience, he had chosen darkness over light. Life and light are the opposite of darkness. Adam's sin brought the darkness and was passed down through every generation, but thank God for a Redeemer filled with life and light in the Blood to overcome darkness and death.

The scripture says as light shines in darkness, the darkness could not understand this light nor put it out. Because darkness is the absence of light, the light will make darkness disappear when it comes on the scene. They

44

cannot exist together. Light always overpowers darkness; darkness never has power over light.

E. God's Expectations

It grieves me to hear men and women say they cannot believe or have faith. It is innate in us to believe or else God would not say to believe Him. He gives us the faith to receive the power to become sons of God. A dark force rules over those who cannot believe and they need deliverance. Christians are the only light unbelievers have and they need someone to show them the pathway to freedom. Jesus Christ went to the cross and died so we could be the lights of the world.

The enemy thought he was snuffing out the life and light, but darkness cannot put out light. Satan thought he overpowered light. When Jesus died and legally went to hell because the sins of the world were placed on Him, being the light that lights every man, His life suddenly came forth. He took away the keys of death, hell and the grave and made a show of Satan openly. As light began to shine, the enemy could not overtake it. Through the death of Jesus, millions of little lights began to explode because Ephesians 1:3 says: "According as he hath chosen US IN HIM before the foundation of the world...." We came forth with Him, raised in the newness of light and life. It is the light the enemy cannot stand. It is the sharp powerful laser beam that can burn through anything.

We cannot be satisfied with the status quo, religious traditions, and how we always do things. We need to be excited in our hearts that God chose us to be vessels through whom He will work in these end times. The Spirit of the Lord wants to show us great and mighty things. God never keeps secrets from His servants on His plans. Jeremiah 33:3 says, "Call unto me, and I will answer thee, and shew thee great and mighty things, which thou knowest not."

We always have to ask ourselves: "How single is my light and am I a light of purity?" We cannot be the light of the world if we are full of different rays of the world's counterfeit or false light, then we are just a false light and filled with darkness. God is always saying to us, "I am a laser beam and I am holy. Now you be holy and don't let in other lights because they will increase your darkness. Allow My laser to stimulate you, not the things in the world. Do not be deceived by those false lights. Let your eye be single and do not let in lights that are really darkness." II Corinthians 11:14 says: "And no marvel. For Satan himself is transformed into an angel of light."

Nothing will take place in your life unless you are willing to be a receiver and apply the truth to your life. Every 'Christian can let their light shine as they believe.

> Arise, shine; for thy light is come, and the glory of the Lord
> is risen upon thee. For, behold the darkness shall cover the

earth and gross darkness the people: but the Lord shall arise upon thee, and His glory shall be seen upon thee. (Isaiah 60:1-2).

God is asking us to receive the fullness of what He did almost 2,000 years ago by the Blood of Jesus and allow our lights to be turned on. God expects something of us in the end times or else He wouldn't have told us to put on the weapons of our warfare and stand. We have the equipment to stop the fiery darts of the enemy, but we need to pull it out of our drawer and use it. End time revival will begin with the knowledge of the Blood of Jesus. We have always had the Blood of Jesus as a weapon, but we have not yet applied it the way we should. The enemy is like a roaring lion seeking the person he can destroy. His whole purpose is to steal the Word sown into the human heart. If you let him have the Word of God in your heart, you will never endure and fight off the attacks of the enemy.

God asks us to let our light shine and have an effect upon our world today. Let's strive to fulfill the scriptures in Matthew 5:14-16.

> Ye are the light of the world. A city that is set on an hill cannot be hid. Neither do men light a candle, and put it under a bushel, but on a candlestick; and it giveth light unto all that are in the house. Let your light so shine before men, that they may see your good works, and glorify your Father which is in heaven.

Chapter Seven

Keeping the Hedge Up

God so loved you that He caused you to be one with Him. Men and women are flesh of His flesh and bone of His bone. We were hidden within Him from the foundation of the world and have now come forth out of Him. We are in Him and He is in us. This same principle was exemplified when Eve was hidden in the side of Adam until God brought her forth and made Adam and Eve one.

Along with washing ourselves with the water of God's Word, we need to understand it is our responsibility to apply the Blood in our lives in order to be overcomers. Revelation 12:11 has to become a revelation in our hearts. "And they overcame him by the Blood of the Lamb, and by the word of their testimony; and they loved not their lives unto the death." Just like Moses stretched out his hand over the Red Sea and caused the walls of water to come down on the enemies of God, you can stretch forth your hand by speaking or applying the Blood over the place where the enemy wants to come against you in your life. Continue your application of the Blood day by day. Just as God used the power of words to create the world, you have the power to speak His Word out of your mouth. Never grow weary in speaking against the adversary as you continue to grow in the Word of God. The Blood of Jesus is "voice activated." Activate its power in your life today.

When the enemy points to you in condemnation and tries to make you back down from your place of authority, say, "This is none of your business. I have Jesus at the right hand of the Father pointing to His Blood on the mercy seat. I am washed by the Blood of the Lamb." Just as the blood in the body cleanses away the carbon dioxide and other wastes, so your sins were cleansed by the Blood of Jesus.

A. Danger of Sin

An unseen enemy is infiltrating our ranks. This enemy subtly wants to deceive us so we will fall away from the faith. Satan targets the saints of God. It is always a trick of the enemy to get us so involved in the world around us that we cannot keep our eyes on Jesus. He draws us away slowly through things such as television or other preoccupations.

Satan wants to steal our time spent in the Word and fill our life with meaningless activities. We have to use effort and set our will to choose God first. He is not going to force us to know Him and spend time with Him; only as we pursue Him will our desires line up with His. Jesus wants a bride without spot or blemish. We have to be pure and holy as He is and not allow such poisons as bitterness and unforgiveness into our Christian lives.

We must guard our hearts and lives against sins that would keep us from operating in our authority. If Satan can gain a foothold in our lives through sin, he can operate legally in our lives. We need to keep our garments washed by the Blood of the Lamb and clean and spotless by an act of our will.

> I beseech you therefore, brethren, by the mercies of God,
> that ye present your bodies a living sacrifice, holy acceptable
> unto God, which is your reasonable service. (Romans 12:1)

God requires holiness and Jesus paid a price for us to walk in that holiness. Jesus agonized in the Garden of Gethsemane where His Blood vessels experienced such stress that His Blood channeled into His sweat glands. He took on our agony, torment, and sin so we could live successfully and holy in this life.

The only way you break the hedge of protection in your life is allowing sin in your life. As long as you ask the Lord to forgive you of the things unpleasant to Him, He will forgive you. I John 1:9 promises, "If we confess our sins, He is faithful and just to forgive us our sins, and to cleanse us from all unrighteousness." If you allow sin in your life, you give Satan legal ground to come in. God has no other choice but to back off and lift His protective hand. It does not matter what the type of sin; sin is sin and when sin invades, it becomes pervasive. When it is confessed, healing comes. We see this principle on a large scale in 2 Chronicles 7:14, "If my people, which are called by my name, shall humble themselves, and pray, and seek my face, and turn from their wicked ways; then will I hear from heaven, and will forgive their sin, and will heal their land." There must be a turning from wicked ways before healing comes. There must be humility and a desire to take authority over the wrongdoing and sin.

Proverbs 3:7-8 admonishes us, "Be not wise in thine own eyes: fear the Lord, and depart from evil. It shall be health to thy navel and marrow to thy bones." Departing from evil is linked to health. The marrow of the bone is the place where blood cells are produced. If you turn from evil and receive the transfusion from Christ's Blood, the Blood of Jesus brings health and life into your bone marrow. Departing from evil and fearing the Lord is a line of defense in itself.

We need to use Psalm 139:1-2 in our lives daily: "O Lord, thou hast searched me, and known me. Thou knowest my downsitting and mine uprising, thou understandest my thoughts afar off." Then Psalm 139:23 and 24: "Search me, O God, and know my heart: try me, and know my thoughts: And see if there be any wicked way in me, and lead me in the way everlasting." As we ask the Father God to search and cleanse us and as we are willing to confess any sin He points out, our hedge will stay intact. The enemy has an advantage over us only when we are not applying the Blood of Jesus and not keeping our heart upright before Him. We cannot mock God. We cannot keep calling Him our Lord if we do not do the things that He tells us to do. God is merciful and long-suffering, but He will not be manipulated.

Smooth talk and clever speech is not the same as an upright heart. You may fool other people, but you cannot fool God. He knows the sins that easily beset you. He knows what wrong things you are not wanting to admit before Him. But when you humble yourself before Him, you will experience peace. Say to Him, "Lord search my heart. I am tired of trying to fool you. Shine your light on me and purge me with your fire." We have all the equipment we need to live a holy life and move into victory in our life. When Jesus died and rose again, the work was finished and completed. We just have to use this finished product in our lives. We cannot cry or lament about what the enemy is doing in our lives as if we have no power to fight him. Of course the same deceiver that spoke to Adam and Eve will come with suggestions like, "Did God really say you can use His authority? Did He really mean that you are not to be moved by what you feel, think or see? Did God really say...?"

B. Danger of Religiosity

Satan is never threatened by a person's religion as long as the person does not have any power in his Christian walk. He does not care how many times a person goes to church, in how many choirs a person sings, or on how many committees a person serves. A Christian is no danger to him as long as God's power is denied in his life. These type of people are described in II Timothy 3:5, "Having a form of godliness, but denying the power thereof; from such turn away."

Many people get caught up in ritualistic practices. Trying to do works in the church is not the way to be spiritual and holy. God does not require works for holiness. Even Adam and Eve tried works to be acceptable with God. The first thing Adam did when he ate from the tree of the knowledge of good and evil was to make a covering for himself with fig leaves. It was not acceptable in the eyes of God and God had to shed the blood of an animal to cover them with an animal skin. He was introducing to them His requirement which is stated in Hebrews 9:22, "...and without shedding of blood is no remission."

Another danger to religiosity is a person's inability to recognize false teaching regarding the Bible. As part of the bride of Christ, we should develop our built-in spiritual detectors to know false doctrine when we hear it. You have to know the Word of God to keep your spiritual ears alive. If you know God's Word, then you will recognize the counterfeit when it comes; but we must realize our minds are not born-again even though our spirits are recreated in the image and likeness of God. Unlike mind sciences which elevate the power of the mind, we as Christians must bring our mind in subjection to the Spirit and Word of God. Romans 12:2 says: "And be not conformed to this world: but be ye transformed by the renewing of your mind, that ye may prove what is that good, and acceptable, and perfect, will of God."

C. Danger of Fruitlessness

As you keep your hedge of protection in place, it is important that you are always bearing fruit as a Christian. Jesus had strong reactions to trees that did not bear fruit.

> And on the morrow, when they were come from Bethany, he was hungry: And seeing a fig tree afar off having leaves, he came, if haply he might find any thing thereon: and when he came to it, he found nothing but leaves; for the time of figs was not yet. And Jesus answered and said unto it, No man eat fruit of thee hereafter for ever. And his disciples heard it. (Mark 11:12-14)

Jesus did not just curse a tree because He was hungry and it lacked fruit. We have to understand that the fig tree in Israel is different than trees with which we are familiar. Fig trees produce leaves and fruit at the same time. Whenever a fig tree has leaves, you automatically know it has fruit to offer. So when Jesus saw the tree from a distance, He had the right to assume that the tree had fruit. Yet, upon closer inspection, the tree only had leaves. The tree had deceived him.

If you go back to biology, a tree with leaves has the ability to make its own food because green plants make their own food through the process of photosynthesis. All the work of a plant is done in the leaves which are the food factory of the plant. Unlike animals who have to go out and find their food, plants can produce their own food. When a tree bears fruit, it does not grow fruit for itself. Fruit is intended to feed others. The tree made its own food and therefore it was selfish.

The fruitless fig tree was essentially saying, "I am going to make my own food, but I am not going to give anything to others." That was unacceptable to Jesus. From the onset of creation, everything was made to reproduce after its kind and told to be fruitful and multiply. The fig tree was in rebellion and disobedience because it had the ability to reproduce fruit and it refused. The reproductive organs are found in the fruit. If the tree bore no fruit, it had no means of reproducing itself. The tree was in rebellion.

The tree was flaunting its leaves which are symbolic of works. We can be in rebellion and do many seemingly Christian works and at the same time not bear true fruit. Fruit never comes because of work—trees do not labor to produce fruit. Fruit is just a product of abiding in the vine. If we abide in Christ and allow the Holy Spirit to dwell in us and have control of our lives, we also bear fruit.

Jesus pointed out an important truth in John 15:1-2. "I am the true vine, and my Father is the husbandman. Every branch in me that beareth not fruit He taketh away: and every branch that beareth fruit, He purgeth it, that it may bring forth more fruit." We should be joyful when the Lord prunes unnecessary twigs out of our lives. It means we will have better fruit and the ability to bring forth more fruit. He goes on to say in John 15:3-4, "Now ye are clean through the word which I have spoken unto you. Abide in me, and I in you. As the branch cannot bear fruit of itself, except it abide in the vine; no more can ye, except ye abide in me."

How then are we able to produce fruit? "But the fruit of the Spirit is love, joy, peace, long-suffering, gentleness, goodness, faith, meekness, temperance: against such there is no law." (Galatians 5:22-23). These fruit will only manifest if we abide in Him—we do not work to produce them. Any branch on a tree which is not connected to the tree eventually withers and dies. It is not receiving the life in the tree. Because of God's grace, we are grafted onto Jesus and become one with Him, just as a branch is grafted onto a tree. Our recreated spirit allows His life to flow through us and bear fruit. As we allow His Blood to flow through us and give us life, our only responsibility is to abide and let the Blood flow and produce fruit. This is like an organ transplant. The transplanted organ only works if the vessels connecting the organ to the body are able to feed blood into it. As blood flows through it properly, it becomes one with the body systems. When the blood vessels that supply the organ with life are not rightly connected, the organ begins to wither and die.

Our Christian life is like an organ transplant. If we take hold of the connection of Jesus Christ and allow the precious Blood to flow through us we will remain steadfast in Him. All we have to do is abide because He gave us everything we need to be overcomers. We just have to activate by faith His life in us because we choose to abide in Him.

D. Tapping Into His Strength

If you understand the agape love of God and the power that accompanies that love, no weapon formed against you will prosper. You have to take the Word of God literally. The Bible is not just good sounding words to glance at occasionally, but words imbued with power and life.

To truly trust the Lord is to grow more childlike. When we ask the Lord what He wants from us, He always says, "Just trust Me." We need to learn to simply trust Him because He said He took our cares. When we feel void of strength, He says He makes us strong. Allow Jesus Christ to strengthen your inner person. Many are being defeated and growing weak and falling at the wayside because they have not tapped into the strength that the Holy Spirit gives. We are "strong in the Lord and the power of His might." (Ephesians 6:10)

Chapter Eight

Becoming a Bride

There is a great significance to the fact that the side of Jesus was pierced on the cross. John 19:34 reads, "But one of the soldiers with a spear pierced His side, and forthwith came there out Blood and water." Although this obscure passage seems tucked in the gospels, the combination of Blood and water was necessary to bring out life. Just as the seed of life was taken from the side of Adam in order to bring forth Eve, Jesus was about to bring forth His bride.

Remember that the life of the flesh is in the blood and that the Blood of Jesus was divine. When His side was pierced, out came the Blood that carried justification and redemption and the water of regeneration that brought refreshing and cleansing. The importance of the water can be seen in Ephesians 5:25-27:

> Husbands, love your wives, even as Christ also loved the church, and gave Himself for it; that He might sanctify and cleanse it with the washing of water by the word, that He might present it to himself a glorious church, not having spot, or wrinkle, or any such thing; but that it should be holy and without blemish.

The water was symbolic of Jesus bringing forth His spotless bride, cleansed by the Word of God. While blood is life being given, we find out that water is a sign of life being received. Jesus was giving life and we are receiving His life. Just like the breaking of the water bag and the coming of water is a sign that a woman is about to deliver a baby, Jesus was about to birth the Body of Christ. We are born of the Blood and water.

God affirms the importance of the water and the blood in I John 5:4-6.

> For whatsoever is born of God overcometh the world: and this is the victory that overcometh the world, even our faith. Who is he that overcometh the world, but he that believeth that Jesus is the Son of God? This is he that came by water and blood, even Jesus Christ; not by water only,

but by water and blood. And it is the Spirit that beareth witness, because the Spirit is truth.

Just as Jesus came by the water and blood, the bride of Christ has come the same way. Ephesians 1:3-5 relates the plan God had for His bride from the beginning of time.

> Blessed be the God and Father of our Lord Jesus Christ, who hath blessed us with all spiritual blessings in heavenly places in Christ: According as He hath chosen us in Him before the foundation of the world, that we should be holy and without blame before Him in love: Having predestined us unto the adoption of children by Jesus Christ to Himself, according to the good pleasure of His will.

Jesus gives us life and the Spirit of Christ brings us forth when a person receives Jesus Christ. Romans 10:9 explains how to receive salvation; "That if thou shalt confess with thy mouth the Lord Jesus and shalt believe in thine heart that God hath raised Him from the dead, thou shalt be saved. "All we have to do is receive a recreated spirit like a woman receives an engagement ring from the man she loves and agrees to become a bride.

A. Bride Coming Forth

We were chosen from the beginning of time to be blessed in Christ. Each one of us has a part of God's character and personality. We are a certain facet of His glory. It is like the different cuttings in a diamond that reflect different rays and colors. If a diamond was only flat, it would never reflect a variety of light. When the whole body of Christ comes together, we will be complete and one with Him and all the rays of light residing in individual Christians will converge to form the pure light of Jesus. We will be His complete body with Jesus as the head. We will come together as a glorious bride exuding splendid rays of life.

We may not look like a bride now, but we will be ready at His coming. God compared the husband and wife relationship to His relationship with the church. He is an anxious bridegroom waiting for the signal from the Father that He can come to earth and get His perfected bride. Jesus was and is the gift given to us from the Father. He is our Savior, Redeemer, King, Sanctifier, and source of power.

The marriage relationship is the institution that foreshadows what Jesus is to His bride, the Body of Christ. I believe that is one of the reasons the enemy is destroying marriages. Satan causes people to lose sight of the preciousness and purpose for marriage. The enemy wants to show that marriage is not what scripture declares it to be so he can take away our understanding of what our relationship should be with Jesus Christ.

I believe the mystery of the Gospel is the mystery of how Christ and the church are related. Ephesians 5:28-32 explains this relationship.

> So ought men to love their wives as their own bodies. He that loveth his wife loveth himself. For no man ever yet hated his own flesh; but nourisheth and cherisheth it, even as the Lord the church: For we are members of his body, of his flesh, and of his bones. For this cause shall a man leave his father and mother, and shall be joined unto his wife, and they two shall be one flesh. This is a great mystery: but I speak concerning Christ and the church.

As we grasp hold of what the Blood of Jesus did to bring forth the bride of Christ, we will begin to come into the perfection that He desires for us. We can never get away from the fact that the Holy Spirit is wooing us into a love relationship with Jesus Christ. He wants us to learn to love Him. God wants a much more mature love from us than the young exciting love of a new bride.

When Jesus asked Peter if he loved Him in John 21:15-17, the word Jesus used for love the first two times He asked was "agape." Agape was unequal to any other love. It came from God the Father and allowed a man to lay down his life for his friends. This word "agape" was never used until the New Testament when Jesus came on earth. This type of love that gives without expecting return has power. We must make a choice to allow this kind of love to flow out of us. As we abide with Jesus on a continual basis, it is easy for this fruit of the Spirit to show forth.

B. Marriage Relationship

God created the reproduction process to be a time of conceiving and bringing forth fruit. Whenever there is an intimate relationship, it is expected that conception will occur. As we spend time with Him, His Word is planted within us and the Word bears fruit. We conceive the seed of the Word as it implants in our spirit and the Word bears fruit.

In the physical realm, the first time a woman has sexual relations there is blood shed. This shedding of blood signifies a covenant between a husband and his bride. There is to be a tie, a binding together through an act of intimacy. They get to know each other in an intimate way. In a spiritual sense, we as the bride of Christ enter into a relationship with Christ and conceive His Word in our hearts. We actually have a blood covenant with Him. He shed His Blood because of His love toward us. To receive Him, we must receive His love and all He provided for us through that love.

C. Covenant Privileges

Understanding the depths of a covenant are crucial to understanding what we have received in Christ. The privileges of a covenant are clearly illustrated in the covenant making of some African tribes. When the famous missionary Stanley needed to travel deeper into Africa, the only way to get through the first tribe he encountered was to enter into a blood covenant with the king of the tribe This required both men to shed their blood and then mingle the two bloods into one to signify their inseparability. Finally, to complete this act, both men would drink the blood, forming a pact by the coming together of the blood. As soon as the men drank the blood, the tribal king began to speak blessings on Stanley that detailed how his life and all his possessions would be blessed. It was law that everything one person owned belonged to the other person who partook of the covenant as well. There also were curses if the covenant was broken.

The prize possession Stanley owned was a milk goat which was important to him because of a stomach ulcer that plagued him. Even though Stanley did not want to surrender his goat, the king wanted it and he could not refuse because of the covenant. In exchange for the goat, the king gave Stanley his spear. Stanley was thinking, "What will this spear do to appease my stomach pains? But I had better abide by the rules of the covenant or I will be cursed."

Stanley traveled on with the spear and a troubled stomach, unaware of his blessings until he met the next hostile tribe who was ready to kill him. But suddenly when the tribesmen saw the spear, they fell on their faces before Stanley. They recognized Stanley was in blood covenant with the same chief with whom they were in blood covenant. Their reverence for the covenant was so great that their hostility was turned to peace and any possession Stanley wanted from the tribe belonged to him. Stanley saw a herd of goats and received back his source of milk.

When we as Christians enter into a blood covenant relationship through Jesus Christ, everything the Father has belongs to us. But sometimes we have to give up our prized milk goats to gain a larger return. If God asks us for the object that brings us pleasure and comfort, we have to realize that God always gives back in abundance what we surrender to Him. Whatever premium we pay, our dividends are going to come back to us because all that He owns is ours. All that He is, we are. The Blood of the covenant lives in heaven's throne room and cries out for mercy.

We break the covenant by sinning, but the covenant is not based on our righteousness. Even when we break the covenant, Jesus comes in and keeps it going because of the precious Blood. The covenant is based on Jesus who shed His Blood for us. Our only requirement is to enter into the covenant and quickly confess sin when it occurs. Every sin in the world is nailed to the cross. He was made sin for us so that our sins would not be counted against us. The Blood of the covenant has set us free so we can enter into His rest and no longer labor with sin. The work accomplished by the Blood means we do not have to work anymore. We are like the tree in Psalm 1:3: "And he shall be like a tree planted by the rivers of water, that bringeth forth his fruit in his season; his leaf also shall not wither; and whatsoever he doeth shall prosper." The work is not ours to do. Fruit simply comes by abiding in Him according to John the 15th chapter.

Christ is the head of His Body. He saved the Body, washed it, and presented it to Himself spotless. We are now a part of His flesh and bones. Jesus fulfilling the roles of Savior, Cleanser, Redeemer, Husband, and Head to us is the mystery of the Gospel, and it is all accomplished through the principle found in Leviticus 17:11: "For the life of the flesh is in the blood: and I have given it to you upon the altar to make an atonement for your souls; for it is the blood that maketh an atonement for the soul." Jesus can be all these things because of the Blood.

I believe God wants us to recapture the perfection of fellowship found in the Garden of Eden. Man was without sin and Adam enjoyed beautiful fellowship with the Lord and exercised dominion and authority over the earth. God does not want us wondering if the Blood has really redeemed us. Jesus opened the way to the inner sanctuary so we could stand in His presence. We have all we need to enjoy an Adam-like fellowship.

When you have a covenant with God, you take on His characteristics and nature. In days of past, the blood covenant was even more sacred than marriage bonds. If a man and woman had entered into a blood covenant, they could not marry or it would be regarded as incest. The covenant had made them like brother and sister. We have a covenant with Jesus Christ and are made one with Him.

D. Importance of Communion

The importance of communion falls into place now that we realize our close relationship to God through our covenant. In John 6:53-56, Jesus addressed His disciples:

> Then Jesus said unto them, Verily, verily, I say unto you, Except ye eat the flesh of the Son of man, and drink his Blood, ye have no life in you. Whoso eateth my flesh, and drinketh my Blood, hath eternal life; and I will raise him up at the last day. For my flesh is meat indeed, and my Blood is drink indeed. He that eateth my flesh, and drinketh my Blood, dwelleth in me, and I in him.

Jesus established communion as a precious sacrament so we would never forget our life comes through eating of His flesh and drinking His Blood. When we partake of communion, we are coming in faith and confirming our belief in what Jesus did for us. It is a fact that what a person eats becomes a part of his physical body. Similarly, if you symbolically eat the flesh of Jesus, you become as He is. If you drink His Blood, you have the life that He has. The physical elements of communion are representative of what happens in the spiritual. We are assimilating into our bodies the oneness we have with Christ. The bread symbolizes the broken body of Jesus and the drink symbolizes His shed Blood.

The scripture warns a person not to take communion unworthily because he is not discerning the Body of Christ. Participating in an unworthy manner brings damnation to a person and causes the sin within him to be energized in a greater manner. In the book of Matthew, Judas finished communion and Satan entered into him. He was taking communion unworthily after Satan whispered in his ear to betray Jesus. He was obeying the devil, the father of death, and his nature came into Judas. The thought of betrayal was not sin had Judas not acted on the evil thought. That which was in him, that sin thought, now became enhanced and Satan was able to possess him. Judas, according to I Corinthians 11:29, was eating and drinking unworthily, and eating and drinking damnation to himself, not discerning the Lord's body.

When you eat and drink of Christ, it energizes the life within you. It is not just a casual ritual to do on a communion Sunday. Do not ever partake of communion unworthily. If you eat unworthily and are full of sin, it re-energizes the sin life within you. That is why every person must examine himself before he comes to the communion and ask forgiveness of any sin. Unbelievers are not to take part in communion because they have not yet asked for forgiveness and allowed the life of Christ to enter in.

There is nothing greater that God wants for us than to enjoy abundant life and be one with Him. He wants us to eat and drink of His eternal life. This desire is revealed in I Corinthians 11:24-26:

> After the same manner also He took the cup, when He had supped, saying, This cup is the new testament in my Blood: this do ye, as oft as ye drink it, in remembrance of me. For as often as ye eat this bread, and drink this cup, ye do shew the Lord's death till He come.

Communion is to be taken as often as you think of Him. As you do, you are injecting His life of healing, reconciliation, redemption, restoration, and provision into your life. Everything that Jesus provided through His body and Blood are yours. You just have to ask: "What do I need the Blood to do for me?" It is like keeping books of coupons that offer all kinds of financial blessings, but you have to know where they are and then redeem them to get the discounts. If you do not know what is in the coupon books, you cannot use them. Everything we need in life is found in Jesus Christ, but if you do not know what is in the Blood, you cannot use it.

Communion allows our body to become one with His. As our hearts are sincere before Him and our sins are confessed, we are worthy to partake and allow the life of Jesus to become real in our bodies. The same life we received when Jesus rose from the dead is incorporated into our physical bodies. Communion brings new life through Jesus's name so we can speak against any kind of affliction that comes against our spirit, soul or body—disease, strife, mental disorders, havoc, and broken relationships. The Blood of Jesus can supernaturally eradicate our enemies.

Through the Blood of Jesus we are brought to the One who nourishes and provides for us. As an adopted child in God's family, we belong to Him. We are joint heirs of Jesus Christ which gives us the rights and privileges He has. The only way we become one with Him is understanding the spiritual law that whatever we eat goes into the body and causes life to be sustained. As we eat His flesh and drink His Blood in communion, His Blood and His life are actually being ingested into us. What is in us is going to be energized and strengthened by His life.

E. Wake Up Call

We are giants in the spirit realm through the benefits of the covenant, but have we been blinded to our greatness? We must awaken this sleeping giant and join together in unity and wholeness. It is our job to encourage and exhort one another to rid the Body of ungodly practices. God does not want to rapture only one individual; He is coming for a Body. One Christian walking right before the Lord is not enough. We must do all we can to get others ready because God wants the whole Body of Christ. That is why the enemy is doing everything he can to keep the body in sin and disunity.

We cannot fulfill the Great Commission or preach the Gospel effectively until sin is out of our lives, yet God has made provision for perfecting the saints. This is found in Ephesians 4:11-13.

> And He gave some, apostles; and some, prophets; and some, evangelists; and some, pastors and teachers; For the perfecting of the saints, for the work of the ministry, for the edifying of the body of Christ: Till we all come in the unity of the faith, and of the knowledge of the Son of God, unto a perfect man, unto the measure of the stature of the fullness of Christ.

We need to hear what the Spirit is saying to the church through the apostles, prophets, evangelists, pastors, and teachers. The Spirit brings forth different messages at different times to bring His people in unity. God always has His fullness of time when He wants things to occur. We need to understand these times and seasons so we can be in line with what He is doing. Jesus cannot come until the bride is perfected and the walls and barriers to that perfection are brought down. When Jesus comes to receive His bride, we are going to be ready for Him by knowing about His Blood.

According to Revelation 22:17, we need to get in agreement with Jesus just as the water and Blood are in agreement. "And the Spirit and the bride say, Come. And let him that heareth say, Come. And let him that is athirst come. And whosoever will, let him take the water of life freely." When the Spirit gets control of His bride and they agree, then the Lord Jesus can come to take us to our heavenly home.

F. Uniting As One

It was not by chance that God calls us a body. The parts of a body have to work together and cannot function unless they are connected together. According to Jesus, membership in the body of Christ is thicker than family blood. In Matthew 12:47-50, Jesus identified Christians over his own family as those with whom He identified.

> Then one said unto Him, Behold, thy mother and thy brethren stand without, desiring to speak with thee. But He answered and said unto him that told him, Who is my mother? and who are my brethren? And He stretched forth His hand toward His disciples, and said, Behold my mother and my brethren! For whosoever shall do the will of my Father which is in heaven, the same is my brother, and sister, and mother.

God makes us a family by the Blood of Jesus. We are made one by His Blood and are not to stay huddled in separate groups or denominations. In the spiritual realm, God only intended one kingdom. Jesus prayed for oneness when on earth, "That they all may be one; as thou, Father, art in me, and I in thee, that they also may be one in us: that the world may believe that thou hast sent me." (John 17:21).

The body of Christ joined together is like a giant puzzle. Each piece of the puzzle is a part of Christ and each new piece is put in place as each new convert comes into the kingdom. Only then do we actually begin to fulfill the command in Genesis to be fruitful and multiply. God is looking to multiply the new life we received from the Blood of Jesus.

Closing

All that we have received to give us life and that life more abundantly was Because of His Blood. The healing, restoration, prosperity, and protection in our lives was Because of His Blood. Our ability to use this end time weapon to come against the devil's kingdom is Because of His Blood. "And they overcame him by the Blood of the Lamb and the word of their testimony..." (Revelation 12:11). This is Blood Power! Because of His Blood!

Postlude

The Bride of Christ is changed because of the Blood. The Blood gives us the opportunity to walk free from sin even as Jesus walked and sinned not. I believe this book is released on the eve of the biggest revival to hit this earth—a revival in which the Holy Spirit is being poured out on all flesh to cause repentance from sin in our lives and a new thirst for Him. May the contents of this book encourage Jesus' Bride to walk in holiness, sanctification, honor, power, and glory. May we be changed by the power of His Blood!

> "But we all, with open face beholding as in a glass, the glory of the Lord, are changed into the same image from glory to glory, even as by the Spirit of the Lord." (II Corinthians 3:18)